100 Ideas for Secondary Teachers:
Geography Fieldwork

Other titles in the 100 Ideas for Secondary Teachers series:

100 Ideas for Secondary Teachers: Outstanding Geography Lessons
by David Rogers

100 Ideas for Secondary Teachers: Outstanding Lessons
by Ross Morrison McGill

100 Ideas for Secondary Teachers: Supporting EAL Learners
by Chris Pim

100 Ideas for Secondary Teachers: Stretch and Challenge
by Paul Wright

100 Ideas for Secondary Teachers: Managing Behaviour
by Johnnie Young

100 Ideas for Secondary Teachers: Tutor Time
by Molly Potter

100 Ideas for Secondary Teachers: Gifted and Talented
by John Senior

100 Ideas for Secondary Teachers: Supporting Students with Dyslexia
by Gavin Reid and Shannon Green

100 Ideas for Secondary Teachers: Revision
by John Mitchell

100 Ideas for Secondary Teachers: Supporting Students with Autism
by Claire Bullock

100 Ideas for Secondary Teachers: Engaging Parents
by Dr Janet Goodall and Kathryn Weston

100 Ideas for Secondary Teachers:

Geography Fieldwork

Fiona Sheriff

BLOOMSBURY EDUCATION
LONDON OXFORD NEW YORK NEW DELHI SYDNEY

BLOOMSBURY EDUCATION
Bloomsbury Publishing Plc
50 Bedford Square, London, WC1B 3DP, UK
29 Earlsfort Terrace, Dublin 2, Ireland

BLOOMSBURY, BLOOMSBURY EDUCATION and the Diana logo are trademarks of Bloomsbury Publishing Plc

First published in Great Britain, 2024 by Bloomsbury Publishing Plc

This edition published in Great Britain 2024, by Bloomsbury Publishing Plc
Text copyright © Fiona Sheriff, 2024

Fiona Sheriff has asserted her right under the Copyright, Designs and Patents Act, 1988, to be identified as Author of this work

Bloomsbury Publishing Plc does not have any control over, or responsibility for, any third-party websites referred to or in this book. All internet addresses given in this book were correct at the time of going to press. The author and publisher regret any inconvenience caused if addresses have changed or sites have ceased to exist, but can accept no responsibility for any such changes

Every effort has been made to trace copyright holders and to obtain their permission for the use of copyright material. The publisher apologises for any errors or omissions and would be grateful if notified of any corrections that should be incorporated in future reprints or editions of this book.

All rights reserved. No part of this publication may be reproduced or transmitted in any form or by any means, electronic or mechanical, including photocopying, recording, or any information storage or retrieval system, without prior permission in writing from the publishers

A catalogue record for this book is available from the British Library

ISBN: PB: 978-1-8019-9481-1; ePDF: 978-1-8019-9482-8;
ePub: 978-1-8019-9480-4

2 4 6 8 10 9 7 5 3 (paperback)

Typeset by Newgen KnowledgeWorks Pvt. Ltd., Chennai, India
Printed and bound in the UK by CPI Group Ltd, CR0 4YY

MIX
Paper | Supporting responsible forestry
FSC® C013604

To find out more about our authors and books visit www.bloomsbury.com and sign up for our newsletters

Contents

Acknowledgements	viii
Introduction	ix
How to use this book	xi

Part 1: Preparing for fieldwork — **1**

1	Increasing fieldwork in your KS3 curriculum	2
2	Fieldwork as part of the hidden curriculum	3
3	The power of a pre-visit	4
4	What's the big idea?	5
5	Location, location, location	6
6	Overcoming trip anxiety	7
7	Sharing information with parents and carers	8
8	What's the risk?	9
9	Period practicalities	10
10	Who ya gonna call?	11
11	StoryMaps	12
12	Residential evening entertainment	13
13	Designing data collection booklets	14
14	Getting the day off to a flying start	15
15	Mission: making memories!	16

Part 2: Fieldwork equipment — **17**

16	Basic fieldwork equipment for your department	18
17	Give it some welly!	19
18	The 'just in case' bag	20
19	DIY fieldwork equipment	21
20	Fieldwork from your phone	22
21	What is this used for?	24
22	Using a weather station	25

Part 3: In the classroom — **27**

23	No equipment, no problem	28
24	Personal mapping	29
25	Perception of crime	30
26	Room with a view	31
27	Sweetie sampling	32
28	Follow the transect, part one	33

29	Using homework	34
30	Sphere of influence	35
31	Virtual fieldwork	36
32	Visit Antarctica and be back in time for break	37
33	Flood risk maps	38
34	Frame it	39

Part 4: On-site fieldwork — **41**

35	Where is the warmest?	42
36	Sit back and look at the clouds	43
37	Lichen and pollution	44
38	How sustainable is your school?	45
39	Soundscaping	46
40	Ecosystems treasure hunt	47
41	Where is our school most likely to flood?	48
42	Simple soil sampling	49
43	Five, six, seven, eight	50
44	Car park surveys	51
45	Follow the transect, part two	52
46	Dandelion or white clover?	53
47	Rahn's Index	54
48	Variations in environmental quality	56
49	Build me a river	58

Part 5: Fieldwork in river environments — **59**

50	The magic of multiple measurements	60
51	Is the bedload boring?	61
52	Rivers bingo	62
53	Dynamic risk assessment	63
54	Kick sampling	64
55	Using rivers for coastal fieldwork	65
56	How does my river flow?	66
57	What is the water quality?	67

Part 6: Fieldwork in coastal environments — **69**

58	Measuring longshore drift	70
59	Groyne profile surveys	71
60	Cliff surveys	72
61	Geology search	73
62	Coastal management survey	74

Part 7: Ecosystems fieldwork — **75**

63	Soil scientists	76
64	Blackthorn, hazel, rosehip ...	77
65	Impacts of coppicing on biodiversity	78

66 Measuring the carbon storage of trees	80
67 Pooters and white sheets	81
68 Country parks and quadrats	82
69 Studying sand dunes and salt marshes	83
70 Pond dipping	84
71 Using the ACFOR scale	85

Part 8: Human fieldwork investigations — **87**

72 How does this place make you feel?	88
73 Graffiti – geography in a spray can	89
74 Supermarket sweep	90
75 Accessibility surveys	91
76 A globalised high street	92
77 Shopping quality index	93
78 Sustainable communities	94
79 Can you see what I see?	95
80 Using local transport for transects	96
81 Pedestrian counts	97
82 Oral geographies	98
83 Perception of safety for women and girls	99
84 Re-photography	100
85 Land-use surveys	101
86 Which way ... that way	102
87 How much is that house?	103

Part 9: Data presentation, analysis and evaluation — **105**

88 What's in a word cloud?	106
89 Radial graphs	107
90 Kite diagrams	108
91 Flowline maps	109
92 Choropleth maps	110
93 Using proportional symbols	111
94 Evaluating methods	112

Part 10: The A Level Geography NEA — **115**

95 Keeping the NEA costs down	116
96 Keeping track of the NEA	118
97 Getting the ethical considerations right	119
98 Pilot study	120
99 How foolproof is your method?	121
100 Evaluating the NEA	122

References — 124

Acknowledgements

I would like to express my sincere gratitude to all of those who have helped to shape my career so far, from my A Level Geography teacher Anna Bass, who helped me more than she will ever know to get through my A Levels; to my ITT mentors Kerrie Brinkley Whittington and Nicola Watson and NQT mentor Karen Wilcox, who let me run with my crazy ideas and never tried to dull my creative spark. To my wonderful colleagues past and present, Amy, Angharad, Elinor, Jema, Jennifer and Sharon, who have been my cheerleaders throughout the past seven years at Kingsthorpe College. Even when they've moved on to pastures new, they have always encouraged me to go further, try harder and never give up. Inspiration is never lacking within our friendship group, and I am incredibly lucky to have you all in my circle.

The geography community is very special, and many of the ideas in this book have been shared by fellow geographers, some of whom I have met, but many of whom I only know through X (formerly known as Twitter). Whilst I may not have met them, they have also shaped my career, strengthened my knowledge and helped me in so many ways. I will forever be grateful to social media for giving me the opportunity to do things such as write this book! A huge thank you to Alice McCaughern, Amy Bunker, Anya Evitt, Brendan Conway, Briley Habib, Catherine Owen, Charlotte Savill, Chloe Searl, Daisy Levett, Fliss Kitching, Dr Helen Renwick, Hilary Carpenter, Iram Sammar, Jess Lomas, Joanne Clarke, Josie Luff, Kate Otto, Kathryn McGrath, Kelly Daish, Kelly Peppin, Lizzie Battrum, Nicola Price, Paul Logue, Rachel Hawke, Sarah Hodges, Stephen Richards, Suzanne Thorne and Tracey Law who have each provided inspiration and ideas for this book. I am glad that I get to share this amazing opportunity with you all. Without geography, I am nowhere, and without the online community I would be lost.

My husband Russell and my two beautiful daughters Isabella and Luna mostly see me work on a plethora of projects and never take a minute's rest. They are my world and everything I do is for them. Here is Mummy's first 'story', Isabella! I wrote this book whilst on maternity leave – thank you Luna for your long naps and cuddles whilst writing.

I also want to extend a huge thank you to Cathy and Joanna at Bloomsbury for this opportunity to share my love of fieldwork and for their constant encouragement and feedback, and to David for his editing work.

Finally, to Fred: a geographer lost, who will be forever 16.

Fiona Sheriff

Introduction

Fieldwork is a hugely important part of the geography curriculum, but due to time constraints it is quite often overlooked. However, without fieldwork, we struggle to develop many of the geographical skills required of students, as geography cannot be learned in the classroom alone.

Since I qualified as a geography teacher ten years ago, the fieldwork requirements at both GCSE and A Level have changed considerably. However, the level of fieldwork training on some ITT courses has decreased, leading to a drop in confidence when it comes to delivering fieldwork. I have spoken to a large number of teachers who have qualified in the last five years: they have felt that they wanted to do more fieldwork, but were not sure where to begin, especially at KS3.

Planning fieldwork enquiries may seem a little daunting, but it needn't be. With fieldwork being a compulsory part of our National Curriculum, GCSE and A Level specifications as well as the International Baccalaureate, it is important that we provide our students with as many fieldwork experiences as we can. We should familiarise our students with the full fieldwork enquiry experience as well as show them just how much we can learn from being outside and putting theory into practice.

This book contains ideas which cover not only the actual fieldwork itself but ideas to help with the planning and preparation around fieldwork, from coasts to urban areas and everything in between, including ideas which can be used on your school site. We all have different environments around us, and I hope some of the ideas here will help to enrich your students' fieldwork experiences, regardless of the school year and stage that they are in.

Hopefully, there is something here for everyone, whether you've just started training or have been teaching for 30 years. But why just trust me with these ideas? I consulted my friends and followers on social media to find the very best ideas, and ones that we know work as they have been tried and tested. Throughout this book are ideas from my geography teacher friends, to whom I am forever indebted, as they have shared so many fantastic ideas which have shaped my teaching practice over the last ten years.

Many of the ideas within this book can be adapted to suit your environment, so don't be afraid to take these ideas and amend them, in fact I actively encourage you to do so. You know your students best, and I look forward seeing how you use these ideas with them to get them thinking like a geographer and carrying out fieldwork in a wide range of environments.

In the online resources there are also links to documents and websites which will hopefully save you time and decrease your workload whilst also helping you to deliver high quality geographical experiences.

As I write this, I am on maternity leave with my youngest daughter Luna, but spending more time in the great outdoors has really cemented my belief in the importance of getting outside. The importance of fieldwork should never be under-estimated, and I hope this book provides you with a plethora of ideas which will help to ignite the fieldwork spark within you.

If you are active on X (formerly known as Twitter), I encourage you to share your experiences using the #100Ideas hashtag, or by tagging me in your posts @fiona_616.

So go on, get outside and let's get fieldwork back on the map!

How to use this book

This book includes simple, practical and tried-and-tested ideas for carrying out geography fieldwork in time-saving, local and low-cost ways to engage and inspire your KS3, GCSE and A-Level students.

Each idea includes:

- a catchy title, easy to refer to and share with your colleagues
- an interesting quote linked to the idea
- a summary of the idea in bold, making it easy to flick through the book and identify an idea you want to use at a glance
- a step-by-step guide to implementing the idea.

Each idea also includes one or more of the following:

> **Teaching tip**
>
> Practical tips and advice for how and how not to run the activity or put the idea into practice.

> **Taking it further**
>
> Ideas and advice for how to extend the idea or develop it further.

> **Bonus idea** ★
>
> **There are 29 bonus ideas in this book that are extra-exciting, extra-original and extra-interesting.**

Share how you use these ideas and find out what other practitioners have done using **#100Ideas**.

Online resources for this book can be found at bloomsbury.pub/100-ideas-geography-fieldwork.

Preparing for fieldwork

Part 1

IDEA 1

Increasing fieldwork in your KS3 curriculum

'I was struggling to think of ideas that naturally fitted into our KS3 curriculum, and I didn't want fieldwork to be just a bolt-on activity. When we sat and really thought about it there were so many opportunities that we had never considered.' *Head of geography*

You do not need to complete an entire investigation at KS3. Instead, you can complete data collection activities or practise fieldwork methods to help strengthen student understanding of fieldwork.

KS3 curriculum time is precious: many schools only offer 1–2 lessons a week, so trying to fit in fieldwork can be difficult. There are many options for simple on-site fieldwork that could be completed in 1–2 lessons:

- **Biomes:** biodiversity study – investigate hedgerows, school playing fields or ways to improve biodiversity on the school site.
- **Weather/climate:** microclimate survey – a great way to learn about different fieldwork equipment as well as collecting a range of data.
- **Plastics:** litter count – where is litter found around the school site? How much is recyclable? What impact is it having?
- **Rivers:** infiltration survey – which surfaces around the school are most likely to flood, and why?
- **Sustainability:** Is your school site sustainable? How could it be improved?

> **Taking it further**
>
> Ask students to carry out similar investigations at home, for example a traffic count. They can then compare this to the school location and ask geographical questions about their data and how the two sites compare. This will also provide a wealth of data to use in the future.

IDEA 2

Fieldwork as part of the hidden curriculum

'Fieldwork provides students with learning opportunities which go far beyond geography content and skills. Careful planning can enhance this learning for our students.'
Catherine Owen, Head of geography

Fieldwork can contribute so much more to our curriculum than just the geography learning that we have planned. We also need to consider the hidden curriculum.

How often do we think about the hidden curriculum? What will our students learn outside our subject area? How will this enhance their understanding of the world and their interactions outside school? This idea from Catherine Owen will help you to consider this.

- Using public transport models more sustainable transport to students and also teaches them how to make the journey, so they can make it independently in the future.
- Many young people have limited opportunities to travel, so fieldwork is a chance for them to develop their confidence in interacting with the wider world.
- Spending a whole day with a group of students gives teachers the chance to engage them in conversations, developing their oracy skills.
- When fieldwork takes place in areas frequented by the public, guidance about appropriate behaviour will influence the way students act. This can be phrased in a positive way, such as 'We are in a large group, but I know you will take care to make sure other people can pass by us and that you will be as well-mannered to them as you are to me'.
- Try virtual visits using Google Street View. In the future, students will be able to use this technique to plan their own outings.

Teaching tip

Provide an email address or an anonymous form so that students can send questions before the trip. Knowing students' concerns can help us to tackle potential problems before they arise.

IDEA 3

The power of a pre-visit

'Carrying out the fieldwork ourselves and thinking like students enabled us to find the pitfalls before taking 100 students out to a location for the first time.' *Head of geography*

If it is your first time carrying out fieldwork or visiting a location it is a good idea to carry out a pre-visit, even if people within your department have been before. Experiencing it yourself may make you see the location in a new light.

Carrying out a trip can be quite daunting, particularly if you have never been to a location before or if it is a new investigation. It is important to know the area, find places for breaks and understand the risks associated with that location.

- Complete the recording sheets you have prepared during your visit. This will help you to ascertain whether data collection is viable and whether the recording sheets work.
- Take photographs. This will not only provide you with up-to-date photographs of the location, but it will also provide your students with an insight into the location – this is particularly important for students who may struggle with external visits.
- Take in the surroundings – is there enough space for a group to collect data without disrupting pedestrians, for example? Or do you need to consider another location?
- Record observations in each location. These can help students to see how a location can change over time.

Teaching tip

Use your data as secondary data for students as you will be collecting data at a different time and on a different day to them. This will provide a useful comparison for students and provide you with data to model with.

Taking it further

Stephen Richards suggests using the pre-visit as an opportunity to find or speak with potential contacts, for example education officers in National Parks.

IDEA 4

What's the big idea?

'For my NEA I found it difficult to decide on an enquiry question, but after carrying out this activity I felt more confident in my title and could easily see the links to the specification.' *Year 12 student*

Deciding on an enquiry question for fieldwork at any level can be difficult, but working through each stage of the question as a group will help you to create the best titles.

Students must consider two key aspects when planning enquiry questions: the geographical and the locational contexts. If either are missing, the question may be too broad and difficult.

Students can use the following process when planning fieldwork enquiries:

1 Consider the underlying themes of your specification. For example, in Edexcel A Level, themes such as causality, systems and interdependence are prominent, and could be investigated. The exam board may have some resources you can use online.
2 Write a brief title giving the theme and the location (e.g. 'To what extent is hard engineering effective in Hornsea?').
3 Share the title with the class or a small team. Is the title specific enough? Does it include a location? Be critical and discuss how to improve it.
4 Now look at the specification. Where does this title fit in? For example, a coastal investigation will quite obviously fit into a coastal systems title. If it doesn't fit the specification, what needs to be changed to make it fit? This process will also make you more familiar with the specification.
5 Re-write your question considering the critique given. Re-share the ideas amongst the class or team until everyone is happy.

Teaching tip

You could use apps or websites such as 'Mentimeter' or programmes such as Google Docs to anonymise the process, particularly if you feel that students may not feel confident in sharing their ideas vocally.

IDEA 5

Location, location, location

'It was really difficult to pick a location for our fieldwork. We had plenty of places to go nearby, but we didn't consider some of the more practical aspects that were important in planning fieldwork.'
ECT1 geography teacher

There are many details to consider when considering a fieldwork location, particularly if it is one you have not visited before. Use online mapping tools to help choose a location and consider the final details of the trip.

No fieldwork location is 100% perfect, but there are certain things to check before carrying out fieldwork (see **Idea 3** for further ideas).

How far away is the location? Use Google Maps to check the distance and timing to check whether the trip is viable within the school day, or whether earlier transport needs to be arranged.

How accessible is the location? Do you have students with specific needs that will need to be taken into consideration? Use Google Maps Streetview to check accessibility. Quite often there are also additional photos embedded into the maps which can help your decision-making.

How many students are you taking? Some locations can be brilliant, but taking more than 60 students can lead to a range of difficulties when choosing access points and data collection sites. Use satellite imagery in online mapping software to help select and measure each site to determine their suitability.

Is there protection from the elements? At a location such as the coast or a rural river, protection from the elements may be difficult and therefore it will be important for students to carry waterproofs with them. Google Maps satellite view may help in assessing this.

Taking it further

Give the questions above to students and show them the location. Can they use Google Maps to answer those questions and critique their fieldwork location?

IDEA 6

Overcoming trip anxiety

'I was so worried about going on a field trip as I hadn't been to the coast before and I didn't know what to expect, but my teachers put my mind at rest and the field trip was really fun.' *Year 12 student*

Students, parents and teachers alike all may struggle with trip anxiety, especially during fieldwork. But what if you could alleviate some of that anxiety with one simple document?

Simplified itineraries that describe the fieldwork in friendly and straightforward language can help to alleviate some of the anxiety that can accompany fieldwork. Joanne Clarke has created a handy document to give to students before the trip that tells them what they need to do the day before and on the day of the trip (see online resources for an example).

- Set up a simple table in a word document which is split into the day before the trip and the day of the trip.
- Break down what needs to be done at each stage – for example, the day before the trip, lay out the clothing needed. In the day of the trip section, detail each stage of the day to make the process that students will go through clear.
- Mention stages of the day where change happens – for example, changing clothes or equipment, toilet breaks and lunch breaks.
- Add a symbol to each stage to summarise the events.
- Print and attach to letters or add to any learning platforms you may use.
- Some students may also be concerned about making time for prayer and their ablutions. Iram Sammar shares how to support your Muslim students on field trips in the document on the online resource centre.

> **Bonus idea** ★
>
> For large field trips and residentials, you could run an engagement session for parents and carers. Show videos and photos of the locations that you are visiting and give information on what happens on a field trip. Parents and carers may then be more likely to provide extra support at home as they will feel empowered to talk about it.

IDEA 7

Sharing information with parents and carers

'Never underestimate the importance of sharing information with parents and carers. You may feel like your instructions are clear but remember that geography is a language all of its own and what us, as teachers, may find straightforward may actually be quite complex for someone who has not had the same experiences.'
Head of geography

Communicating with parents and carers is important. They may not be aware of the practical elements around fieldwork nor the clothing requirements if they are not suitably informed.

Fieldwork is a huge part of the GCSE and A Level specifications and is therefore compulsory, but how many parents and carers are fully aware of the requirements before their children start the course? These simple ideas could help to increase parental understanding and engagement around fieldwork.

At the GCSE and A Level introduction/options evenings provide a leaflet giving information about the fieldwork requirements to make clear the prices, locations and aims. Also make clear any support that parents can receive regarding the cost of fieldwork. See the online resources for an example.

As **Idea 6** suggests, sharing a simple and straightforward itinerary with parents giving full details of the day could help to alleviate any fears that they may have.

Most schools have a text or email system that can send whole cohort messages easily, without extra work for you. Ask your school office to send a message the day before the trip to remind parents of key details such as timings, lunch, equipment and clothing.

> **Bonus idea** ★
>
> If you have someone particularly tech-minded in your department, or a student who enjoys making videos, put together a short video that shows what happens on a fieldwork trip so that parents can further understand the requirements of the day.

IDEA 8

What's the risk?

'Whilst risk is not the most interesting part of the planning process, it is the most necessary.' *Educational visits co-ordinator*

Risk assessments are an important part of the fieldwork process, but they can be tricky to get right. Where can you seek advice?

Taking pupils out of the classroom into the field involves inherent risks, but these risks are important to child development. Outdoor learning can have positive impacts on academic achievement, behaviour and personal development and we have a statutory duty to provide two opportunities for fieldwork at KS4. Suzanne Thorne shares her ideas on where to seek advice on writing a good risk assessment.

The Outdoor Education Advisers' Panel (OEAP) offers national guidance for planning and conducting fieldwork in a range of environments and on a range of factors which could impact on risk. Document 7.1h 'Field studies' offers guidance ranging from weather and group safety to external providers and working near water. Document 3.3e 'Checklist for visit planning' offers support to ensure that everything has been considered and planned for.

Access to the OEAP national guidance documents is free: https://oeapng.info/. You can also ask your school educational visits co-ordinator (EVC) for support as it is their role to ensure trips are conducted safely.

Look at your existing school paperwork for risk assessments. It is likely these can be amended and used for your fieldwork. There may be generic risk assessments for factors such as transport, and specific risk assessments for individual locations.

> **Bonus idea** ★
>
> Practise writing a risk assessment for a trip without first looking at existing ones. Can you identify the risks and suggest mitigations for them? You could also get your students to practise writing a risk assessment, especially your NEA students as they will need to complete one as part of their write-up.

IDEA 9

Period practicalities

'Whilst our field trips are short, you may be far from toilets or changing rooms. Giving simple advice to your students can help to ensure that they feel comfortable completing fieldwork.'
Head of geography

Menstruation is still often a taboo subject, but it shouldn't be. How do we ensure that students feel comfortable in the field dealing with their periods?

Fieldwork and menstruation can be a difficult combination and can feel like a barrier to completing fieldwork. With a few key pieces of advice for students they will all hopefully feel comfortable and therefore less likely to dodge fieldwork if they are worried about it.

If you don't feel comfortable talking about periods, ask someone in your department who does and observe them whilst they speak to students about it. This will help you form your dialogue for future conversations.

Speak to your students about options for menstruation products such as menstrual cups and 'period underwear', as these can usually be worn for longer if your fieldwork is lengthy. These products are particularly useful where access to toilets may be limited, and students may feel worried about regular access to them.

Ensure that you have period products, wet wipes and hand sanitiser in your bag, and let students know that you are carrying these with you. The more periods are talked about, the less taboo they become. Preparedness in this area will help students who are participating in the Duke of Edinburgh award.

A useful document to help when talking to your students about periods and fieldwork can be found in the online resources.

> **Teaching tip**
>
> Many female scientists have now written blogs on this topic and it is worth sharing those with students to give real-life examples to students on this matter. These could be shared on your online learning platform for students to read at their own leisure.

IDEA 10

Who ya gonna call?

'The importance of this document came to fruition when we were broken down on the way back from a trip, my phone had run out of battery and others had no signal to get onto our school management information system. Thank goodness we had important details written down.' *Geography teacher*

A must-have document in your teacher packs is a list of emergency contact details and instructions. Many of the details, such as accommodation, can be written and printed once, and then updated with student contact details for each trip.

Putting together an emergency contact list is really simple but really important. Some systems such as Arbor and SIMS can put together these lists for you. It is vital that these are printed and given to each member of staff, and then destroyed after each trip for GDPR purposes.

Each school will have their own requirements, but below is a basic list of what you should include in your emergency document to ensure that you have the details that you need in any eventuality:

- contact details of at least two people for each student whom you could contact in an emergency
- allergy and medical information for each student
- emergency contact details for the school, including an out-of-hours number
- details of the venue or provider that you are using
- details of the coach company, including an out-of-hours number
- if using a school minibus, also include details of the breakdown assistance and bring the fuel card.

Teaching tip

For NEA students, ask them who they think should be included in this document. You could ask this when students are completing their own risk assessments.

IDEA 11

StoryMaps

'Our teacher set up an ArcGIS StoryMap and it was so helpful in reminding us what we did for our fieldwork as well as how to link it to exam questions.' *Year 10 student*

ArcGIS StoryMaps are not only a great way to bring together different areas of student fieldwork, but also to upload data to once fieldwork is complete. I tell students that our ArcGIS StoryMaps will be their new best friend when it comes to revising their fieldwork.

ArcGIS is free for schools to access, and it is a great tool to set up StoryMaps, which can help students in a number of ways. ArcGIS allows you to share maps and data, but also to include narrative and multimedia content such as videos and photographs. These can be set up before going on fieldwork and then added to once data has been collected. See the online resources for an example.

- Start with writing your aims and hypotheses in a text box on StoryMaps, and explain why these have been chosen.
- Add a map of the location and pinpoint the sites, adding a narrative to each site. You can also add photographs to each site for further clarity.
- Add photographs or short video clips of the different equipment and fieldwork methods underneath your map and hypotheses.
- Include links to websites containing secondary data such as crime information or the 2021 census.
- Once the fieldwork has been completed, add maps with imported data from ArcGIS. Now all of your maps and data will be in one place and students can revisit this throughout their revision.

Taking it further

Students could create their own ArcGIS StoryMaps for their second piece of fieldwork. Not only will this be a great way to trial GIS with GCSE students, it will also test their understanding of the fieldwork process and be a great way for them to revise what they did. These can then be kept for the following years' students to access as secondary data.

IDEA 12

Residential evening entertainment

'Having plans for the evening ensured that our students made the most of their field trip and minimised any potential issues.'
Assistant principal

Residential trips are a great way to cover a range of fieldwork opportunities, but how do you keep students busy in the evening?

If you are lucky enough to be able to run a residential field trip you may be wondering what to do in the evening with your students. Some centres will have their own activities which you can book in advance; others may only provide accommodation. Evening activities help to build relationships and keep students busy.

- Before you go, ask students to create ten quiz questions – these could be individual or group questions depending on group size. You can then put these together for an evening quiz with little preparation work as it has been done by the students. An example quiz can be found in the online resources.
- Go on a walk. Get to know the area around your accommodation. Remind students to take lots of photographs as these could be used as part of their fieldwork write-up. Remember to write this into your risk assessment.
- Set a challenge. Before you go, you could plan challenges, such as taking A–Z photographs, a scavenger hunt or even making a video about their fieldwork experience for the next cohort. Creativity will certainly keep students busy.
- Students could also complete parts of their write-up – for example, evaluating their methods whilst they are still fresh in their minds or annotating photographs on mobile phone apps if they do not have a laptop.

Teaching tip

Keep copies of any activities that you create so that they can be used again with the next cohort. This also includes quiz questions that students have created. This will save time in your planning.

IDEA 13

Designing data collection booklets

'Invest the time into creating them as once they are complete you'll be able to use them again and again.' *Head of geography*

Data collection booklets are a staple in fieldwork as they keep all of your students' data in one place. They can be tricky to put together and a little time-consuming, but the time invested in their creation will be worthwhile!

Fieldwork is a great opportunity for worksheets to go flying! I've seen it happen many times, especially when the wind picks up at the coast. Creating a data collection booklet will help to eliminate this as booklets keep everything in one place and are less likely to be lost than individual worksheets. See the online resources for an example booklet.

Start by creating a page for students to fill in which recaps their aims, enquiry questions, hypotheses and methods. Students can then read or complete this on the coach or at the first location. Include a map of the location and the sites for students to refer back to.

Divide your booklet up by site rather than method. This will help students to easily find each table that they need to fill in rather than flicking through lots of pages each time. If will also help teachers to see if students are missing any data.

Include a space for notes in each section of the booklet, where students can write down any observations for each site as well as answers to any questions they might ask.

If re-photography (see **Idea 84**) is one of your methods, include photos in the booklet so that they don't get lost. It will also remind students to take photographs where needed.

Taking it further

Ask your GCSE students to design their own data collection sheets which could be used in the booklet. This will save you time in their creation and they can then evaluate their data collection sheets following the fieldwork.

IDEA 14

Getting the day off to a flying start

'A smooth start to the day is a stress-free start to the day, always important with fieldwork.' *Geography teacher*

Fieldwork can be stressful, but a little organisation can help to reduce stress levels and get the day off to a flying start.

I always have the same routine, which begins the week before the trip. Being organised is important, and once you've led a trip for the first time you'll find your own way to get the day off to a flying start. Until then, this process may help!

The week before, ensure that any free school meals have been ordered so that they can be picked up on the day of the field trip. Have all of the paperwork printed, such as risk assessments, student lists and work booklets. Print a few more booklets than are needed, in case one blows away or gets left on the coach.

A few days before the trip, arrange a meeting with all of the attending staff and delegate jobs such as picking up the first aid kit, collecting work booklets and giving out clipboards.

The day before, make it clear to students and parents where the meeting point is and what time you'll be meeting. Also let form tutors know to send students to you in the morning if they happen to appear in the classroom instead.

On the day, give copies of the register to all staff. This should include medical information for each group. Take a stash of stationery down to your meeting point. If students are in non-school uniform they may have forgotten to bring a pen.

Smile! Once everyone is in the right place, share your expectations and have the best day.

Teaching tip

Set up a checklist for all of the jobs that need completing before the trip. Arrange it by date and time to keep you organised in the week leading up to the trip.

IDEA 15

Mission: making memories!

'Remember, you're making memories! Field trips are often the times children talk about and remember, so make sure it's enjoyable.'
Nicola Price, learning leader for geography

Make sure you build in some memory-making alongside the brilliant geography.

Consider your context. For me, this includes understanding how some students have a very small local sphere, with no concept of the local river, or beach, or maybe the next town.

Field trips can be about creating core memories, with some skills thrown in along the way. Nicola Price shares some ideas as to how she's built this into her fieldwork trips.

These trips break up the predictable, safe routine of the classroom and are memorable – they don't need to be far-flung, or involve the latest hi-tech fieldwork sampling equipment.

- Taking students to the coast for salt marsh and sand dunes studies, I pick a local coastal resort. Students identify vegetation species, measure sand dune transition, then buy ice-cream and play rounders on the beach. They remember the trip to the seaside, the experience of clambering the dunes and spotting birds in the saltmarshes, even if it did rain all day!
- The looks of awe and wonder when visiting a city museum are worth every bit of the deluge of paperwork that accompanies organising field trips, especially when a student tells you they've never set foot in a museum before. No pieces of equipment are required, beyond a pen and pencil!
- Woodland studies at a local activity centre allowed Year 10 to survey vegetation cover and variety across the site and finished off with a session of grass sledging!

Taking it further

You could create a geography 'bucket list'. This could be 20 things you think geography students at your school should do before they have finished their education with you.

Part 2

Fieldwork equipment

IDEA 16

Basic fieldwork equipment for your department

'When I first started we didn't have any equipment at all in our department. Over the years we have built up a supply, but I wish there had been a basic list when I first started teaching.'
Geography teacher

There is no 'one size fits all' when it comes to geography fieldwork equipment, but this list may give you an idea as to the types of equipment you may need to help students to develop their understanding of the world around them.

Following this basic list of equipment will help you to carry out a range of investigations both on your school site and in the wider area. You could also ask your school's Science and Maths departments as they may have some of this equipment already and may be willing to lend it to you. Check out **Idea 19** for some DIY versions of these equipment suggestions:

- thermometers, anemometers, compasses, and rain gauges for weather recording;
- measuring tapes, trundle wheels and stopwatches for basic quantitative data collection;
- plant and insect identification guides and quadrats for ecosystems investigations;
- infiltrometers for infiltration investigation;
- calipers for measuring sediment size;
- clinometers and ranging poles for measuring gradient.

Having a few of each item will help hugely in diversifying the range of fieldwork options available to your classes. However, there are also many options for fieldwork which do not require specialist equipment if your budget will not reach to buying these pieces, such as a sustainability survey or traffic count survey.

Taking it further

Before using the equipment, give each piece to students and ask them to guess what they are used for or ask them to list as many uses as they can for each piece of fieldwork (see **Idea 21**). This fun activity could lead to further fieldwork ideas for your classes.

IDEA 17

Give it some welly!

'Working in an area of deprivation meant that many students did not have access to basic fieldwork clothing such as wellies and raincoats. We asked for contributions from our community and now have a healthy stock of waterproofs perfect for fieldwork.'
Amy Bunker, assistant principal

Wellies, waterproof jackets, waterproof trousers and waders are all useful clothing to take on fieldwork, but our budgets may not stretch to buying them, and many students will not have their own. This idea will help you to solve this issue.

How can we ensure that our students have suitable waterproofs without spending our entire department budget on them? Amy Bunker and Kelly Daish share their ideas on how to build your supplies:

- Put a note out to all staff asking for donations of wellies, walking boots and waterproofs.
- Try the power of social media: many people have waterproofs and wellies gathering dust in their garages and would love to put these to good use. Local selling pages are a great place to start asking.
- Try local sponsorship. Companies might want to sponsor the purchase of a few pairs of wellies or waterproof trousers, particularly if their staff have children at your school.
- Get friendly with the staff running the Duke of Edinburgh Award or the Combined Cadet Force (CCF) as they may have similar equipment that they could lend to you.

Teaching tip

Ask students what equipment they think they might need and why it's important. Look at weather forecasts and photographs of the area to provide inspiration.

Bonus idea ★

Make a note of all of the sizes of wellies and waterproofs and create a sign-out sheet so that you know what has been lent out and who to. Let parents know that this equipment is available to students to alleviate their concerns about having to buy waterproofs.

IDEA 18

The 'just in case' bag

'Miss always seems to have everything we need with her, plasters, safety pins, rain ponchos … she has everything in that bag of hers.'
Year 10 student

Just call it a Mary Poppins bag for fieldwork! A bag of odds and ends and everything you need to make the day run smoothly.

In my classroom I keep a bag of equipment to be taken on fieldwork. It isn't necessarily fieldwork equipment, but rather things that have come in useful to solve issues or make fieldwork easier:

- £1 rain ponchos – useful for students missing waterproofs, covering rucksacks in downpours or a lunchtime sit!
- Spare change for the toilets – having loose change in my bag has saved the day on numerous occasions.
- Spare stationery – you'd be surprised at how many pens and pencils get lost in one day!
- A quick-dry camping towel – for when a student becomes completely drenched in the river and didn't bring a spare change of clothes.
- Two sun hats – you can guarantee that a student or two will forget their sun hat. The floppy bucket style hats are perfect as they are quick-drying, comfortable, keep the sun off the students' heads and take up little room in your bag.
- Two pairs of socks – for those students who wore wellies with holes in!
- Safety pins – for the raincoat zips that fail.
- Spare cutlery – for the students who forget theirs but brought pasta for lunch.
- Cereal bars, dried fruit and boiled sweets – a sweet treat for when energy is low.
- Ball of string – for measurements, or to fix bags, tie up sleeves or adapt quadrats.

Bonus idea ★

At A Level, ask students what equipment they think they might need to take with them on their fieldwork to solve problems. They may have ingenious solutions to problems that could arise.

IDEA 19

DIY fieldwork equipment

'Sometimes you have to get a little bit creative in fieldwork.'
Head of geography

In an ideal world we would have a cupboard full of fieldwork equipment that we could use as and when we want, but for many of us this isn't a reality. This problem can be partially solved with a few home-grown solutions.

Making your own fieldwork equipment could be one way to ensure that your classes can participate in fieldwork, therefore a little trip to your local DIY stores and charity shops might be in order! Catherine Owen shares two great ideas for some DIY fieldwork equipment:

- Wire coat hangers can be bent into squares to create quadrats. These can be placed on the ground in contrasting locations around your school site to investigate biodiversity and species cover.
- Find a small section of drainpipe in your local DIY store or from your site staff and cut it into 15 cm lengths using a craft knife or a saw. These lengths can be turned into infiltrometers to investigate infiltration. Mark centimetre measurements along the length of the drainpipe using a permanent marker Then place it on the ground (if it's concrete) or push 1 cm into the ground if it is grass/sand and pour in water until it reaches the 10 cm mark. Time how long it takes for the water to soak into the ground.

The Met Office website also has a range of ideas on how to make simple weather recording equipment such as rain gauges and anemometers (search for 'Make your own weather station'). These could be made for a homework task to enable students to collect weather data at home.

Taking it further

If you have a geography club in school you could run an activity where students are given a range of recyclable materials and asked to design their own fieldwork equipment. This is a great way to challenge their creativity and test their problem-solving skills.

IDEA 20

Fieldwork from your phone

'Using my phone to collect fieldwork data was far more practical than having lots of data collection sheets. It also meant that I could easily upload it to spreadsheets rather than writing it out by hand.'
Year 12 student

Using modern technology is a great way to capture data, especially when photographs are geotagged, and data can easily be imported. Having online data cuts down the time taken to present data, leaving students more time for analysis.

There are now many apps that can be used by geography students and teachers that either provide useful information about a location or allow you to collect data and upload it into programmes such as ArcGIS. Here are some example tried-and-tested apps that are great for fieldwork.

- Data recording: GeogIt contains over 30 fieldwork methods including soundscaping and activity mapping. There are a range of both human and physical methods available, and this data can be exported straight into Excel which can then be uploaded to ArcGIS. The latitude and longitude of each data collection site is recorded, making it easy to geolocate data.

- Survey app: Survey123 is a mobile app extension of ArcGIS which allows you to collect data which can be imported straight into ArcGIS to create a beautiful, located data presentation. Students will need an ArcGIS log-in to set up their own surveys, but they can also use QR codes to download surveys set up by teaching staff.

- Light intensity recorder: Lux Meter can be used to measure light intensity as part of a microclimate survey.

> **Teaching tip**
>
> Practise using these apps in school before you leave for fieldwork. Many of these apps will work well for on-site fieldwork, adding a new technological dimension to fieldwork.

> **Taking it further**
>
> Discuss the advantages and disadvantages of using mobile apps for completing fieldwork with students. The discussion can feed into their evaluation and get them thinking about the most efficient and accurate way to collect fieldwork data.

- Decibel gauge: Decibel X:dB can be used to measure sound levels as part of a human geography investigation.
- Soil information: mySoil is a British Geological Survey app containing information about soil types in your area.
- Place identification: what3words is great for NEA fieldwork as you can specifically locate places with ease, giving them a three-word identifier.
- Mapping tool: OS Locate is a free compass and grid reference tool, giving eastings and northings as well as your altitude.
- Recording routes: Simple Logger is an app which will allow you to record your route, add notes and photographs and track changes in elevation. This data can then be uploaded to Google 'My Maps'.
- Oral geographies: With permission, students could record conversations held to create oral geographies. These can be recorded using a voice notes app. Many voice notes apps also capture the location of the recording.
- Measuring: Most smartphones will have an inbuilt measuring app. These are useful when students want to take a measurement but don't have a measuring tape. The app may also measure angles so could be used as a makeshift clinometer.

IDEA 21

What is this used for?

'This was a really fun activity, a bit like *Guess Who?* for fieldwork equipment.' *Year 7 student*

Students need to know what different fieldwork equipment is used for, before they use it, and this can easily be carried out in the classroom using the physical equipment or as a card sort activity. This is also a great way to improve students' use of geographical vocabulary.

Teaching tip

Put a large timer onto the board so students can see how much time they have left. The noise level might increase as the timer runs out, but students will be excited to find out what each piece of equipment is used for.

If you are fortunate enough to have a range of fieldwork equipment in the classroom, this is a great activity to get students guessing about what each piece is used for. This activity can get a little noisy, but it is always a fun way to gauge student understanding around fieldwork equipment.

- Sit the students in groups and set up a table at the front of the room with a range of equipment laid out on top of it. Don't put the names of the equipment onto the table.
- Groups can send up one student at a time and they need to look at the equipment and then go back to their groups and describe one piece of equipment they saw. The remaining students on the table need to guess what piece of equipment they are talking about, name it and describe its use.
- Give students a clear time limit. Can they name and describe all of the pieces within the set time?

If you don't have the equipment, you could give students a set of photograph cards and a set of descriptions. Students need to match the descriptions with the photographs to guess the name and use of each piece of equipment. See the online resources for an example.

IDEA 22

Using a weather station

'We built our own Stevenson Screen to take weather observations. It also meant we could carry out regular fieldwork and practise data presentation in a meaningful way.' *Sarah Hodges, geography teacher*

Weather stations, whether home-made or purpose built, are a great way of collecting continuous data which can be used in a variety of ways.

Sarah Hodges has created a brilliant weather station with her students using inexpensive or recycled materials alongside weather equipment. Instructions on how to build a simple weather station can be found in the online resources. Purpose-built weather stations can also be purchased and set up to collect data.

Weather stations and the data they produce can be used in a range of different ways:

- Introduce students to the types of equipment that meteorologists use when forecasting the weather. You could provide a hands-on experience on how the weather equipment works.
- In a weather topic, compare weather forecasts with the information produced by the weather station. What similarities and differences are there? Assign a different student each lesson to read information from the weather station; this will also help to improve geographical literacy.
- Use the data collected over a week or month to practise data presentation – for example, drawing a line graph to show changes in temperature.
- Keep a weather log using the data and add day-to-day observations, such as when there was rain, a storm or snow.

Taking it further

Set up a meteorology club in school to encourage further fieldwork. This could include students completing frequent microclimate data collection or uploading the data onto your school website. They could find schools in other areas with similar projects to share data with.

In the classroom

Part 3

IDEA 23

No equipment, no problem

'I didn't think I would be blowing bubbles in a geography lesson!'
Year 7 student

With dwindling school budgets, fieldwork equipment is usually a fairly low priority, but not all fieldwork requires specialist or fancy equipment. Sometimes, keeping it simple is the best way.

A simple microclimate investigation can be carried out on your school site using equipment you may already have, can buy cheaply or can borrow from the science department. The ideas below require: a smart phone or tablet, bubbles, cardboard grid, thermometer and empty drinks bottles.

- Download a luxmeter onto a **smart phone or tablet** to measure light intensity. Use this to capture information about sunlight and shade at each site. Data could be captured using Survey123.
- Stand into the wind and blow **bubbles** to get a rough idea of the wind direction. Use the compass app on a **mobile phone** to assess the wind direction.
- Make a **cardboard grid** (see online resources for a template) and hold it up to the sky to collect data on cloud cover. For example, if two squares have cloud cover in them you would say there is 2/8 cloud cover.
- Use a **thermometer** to give an indication of the temperature in each location. This could also be compared to temperature data on a **mobile phone** for your location.
- Create a rain gauge using **empty drinks bottles**. Cut off the top of the bottles and mark millimetres on the side using a ruler. Place the bottles around the school site and collect data at the end of the week. Instructions for this can be found in the online resources.

Bonus idea ★

The Royal Meteorological Society run a free equipment borrowing service, all you need to pay is the return postage. Search for 'Borrow an instrument'. This includes digital equipment to help you to collect accurate data.

IDEA 24

Personal mapping

'This was a great introduction to fieldwork for our Year 7s.'
Geography teacher

Maps and an understanding of place are a good entry point to introducing fieldwork to your students. Starting with their own personal geographies enables your students to show you their mapping skills at an early stage.

Personal mapping or 'mental maps' are a way for students to demonstrate their perception of a location. These could be maps of their route to school, their favourite local places or a map of an area they enjoy visiting. They are drawn from the students' own memory, and offer an insight into their knowledge of maps, cartographic skills and whether they have any misconceptions of a location.

Start with a discussion as to what a personal map is. You could draw an example of a map personal to you – for example, your local area or the area around the school. This could be a map from a bird's-eye view or you can play with the scale and sketch key features that are important to you.

Ask students to draw their personal maps. You could give the class the same task – for example, drawing their route to school.

Model how to add annotations to a map and then ask students to add annotations to their own maps. Show the best examples under a visualiser to share best practice.

Remind students to add vital map features such as a title, north arrow, key and colours.

Once complete, show a map of the local area on your screen, and ask students which features they have included on their maps. Circle them on the screen.

Teaching tip

This activity could be used as a transition activity with Year 6 or as a first activity with Year 7. This will enable you to establish a baseline as to their cartographic skills.

Taking it further

Look at which areas are unknown on the map to your students. These could then form the basis of a local fieldwork investigation.

IDEA 25

Perception of crime

'Accessing crime data really made us think about how different parts of our town are perceived.' *Geography teacher*

Students need to access a range of secondary data sources. Investigating crime data and perceptions of crime will enable your students to use GIS, maps of different scales and a variety of mapping techniques in the classroom.

Secondary sources of data are not only useful for comparisons in geography, but they also enable students to access data that they would struggle to collect first hand. One example of this is crime data. How you approach using crime data will depend on the age and maturity of your class. Remember that this may need to be handled sensitively depending on your local context.

At KS3 you could investigate perceptions of crime:

- Enlarge maps of parts of your town to A3 and lay them out on the tables. Give students three colours or coloured stickers, Use one colour to indicate areas where they feel safe, one colour to indicate areas where they don't feel safe and one colour to indicate areas they don't know.
- Students should look at each map and circle areas they perceive to have a high level or crime. They can write their explanations down by annotating the map.
- When complete, show students each map under the visualiser. Students should write about the patterns that they see – why do some areas feel safer than others?
- This can then be compared to data on the police website to see if their perceptions of crime match what is happening in their town: www.police.uk/pu/your-area/.

Taking it further

At KS4, students could use the police website themselves to see where the largest numbers of crime happen, or the data could be provided in table format. This data could then be turned into a chropleth map or proportional symbols used to practise data presentation techniques.

Bonus idea ★

You could provide students with photographs of crimes such as vandalism or graffiti which have been used in the media. Students could annotate these photographs to explain what they see and how this makes them feel.

IDEA 26

Room with a view

'I didn't appreciate just how much geography we could see from our window; it's amazing when you really look.' *Year 11 student*

Field sketches are one of those skills that you can easily practise in your classroom. Use the view from your classroom windows to evaluate this geographical skill within a lesson time. Perfect for a rainy day!

From my classroom window I can see features that are often overlooked by my students – for example, the local housing estate, trees and hedgerows and, in the distance, wind turbines. Many of these features are completely missed by students as they are part of their everyday geographies.

- Model the process (for help, see the online resources). Showing students how to divide their page and how to decide what to draw first will enable them to approach their field sketch in an organised manner.
- Give each student paper and a clipboard and ask them to stand in front of the window. If you only have small windows or a view into the corridor, select a different site around school or take students outside to practise.
- Ask students to point out what they can see and whether these are human or physical geography features. Remind them to point out even the most obvious features.
- Give students 10–15 minutes to draw their field sketch. They should also include annotations.
- Once complete, ask students to return to their seats and to evaluate the technique. They should be able to tell you the advantages and disadvantages of field sketches. Ask them how they would improve this technique.

Taking it further

Ask students to complete the same activity at home, either drawing field sketches from their own windows, or by drawing their view outside. Students can then compare their field sketches in a variety of locations and get a little more practice in.

IDEA 27

Sweetie sampling

'I found the different types of sampling difficult to understand, but this activity helped me to understand each type, and how best to use sampling strategies in my NEA.' *Year 12 student*

Learning the different types of sampling can be quite complicated, but this fun activity using sweets or coloured counters is an effective method of differentiating between sampling methods in a memorable and light-hearted way.

Teaching tip

Using coloured counters avoids waste, and these can be used year after year and stored in envelopes or containers. You could also follow this activity with sets of data to put theory into practice.

There are lots of incarnations of this activity online and there is a worksheet you can use on the online resources. To run this activity without sweets you could also use coloured counters from the maths department.

- Divide the sweets or counters into containers and share these between the groups in your class. Ideally, there should be around 30 sweets or counters in around five colours for each group.
- Ask students to divide the items into their different colour groups, count them and work out the percentage of each colour – this will give you the target population.
- Line up the items, close your eyes and pick ten at random, writing down the number of each colour picked. This represents random sampling.
- Line up the items again and divide the total number by ten. Count along the line in this number – for example, if you had 30 sweets, you would note down the colour of every third item. This represents systematic sampling.
- Look at your target population: you now need to create a sample of ten that represents the target. For example, if 25% of your target population were red, you would need 25% of your sample to be red. This represents stratified sampling.

IDEA 28

Follow the transect, part one

'This is a great way to practise three ideas at once: land use surveys, some basic GIS and transects.' *Geography teacher*

A transect is a line along which measurements or data are taken. Practising using a transect can be done through using websites such as Google Maps, choosing a range of locations and seeing how they change along the transect. This can then be combined with other geographical skills.

You will need access to computers or tablets. If you have access to Digimaps you could also print blank base-maps of the location you want to practise this skill in (e.g. a high street).

- Introduce students to a transect and a land-use survey (see **Idea 85**) and explain to students that they will be completing a virtual land-use survey along the transect.
- Using Google Maps, students should start their transect at the chosen point and note down the type of building. Doing this along a high street will give a range of shops and vacant buildings.
- Students can either practise systematic sampling, noting down the land use of every fifth building, or note down the land use of each building.
- Using GIS they can create a land-use map. ESRI have a great guide on this online.
- This can then be moved to a larger scale and students could look at how land use changes from the Central Business District (CBD) to the suburbs, drawing a straight line on the map and recording how the land use changes along the transect.

Taking it further

Ask students to complete a different type of data presentation. This will open up a dialogue about what type of data presentation is best for each data type. For example, land use could be tallied and turned into a pie chart or bar chart instead of creating a land-use map.

IDEA 29

Using homework

'I usually hate homework, but I found this interesting as it made me look harder at the area around me.' *Geography student*

Using homework is a great way to encourage students to collect data about their local area, practise essential fieldwork skills and further understand secondary data.

Homework is used in many ways to further student experiences in fieldwork. In lockdown, my team created an investigation that students could complete at home and then send their results into school. Students were set a range of activities to investigate their 'place' and then compare it to others' in the class. This could be set as a homework project for a term.

Students can complete the activities below independently using the materials provided in the online resources:

- Field sketches outside their window or in a local park.
- Environmental quality survey in their local area – these could be repeated in a range of contrasting locations.
- Radial diagrams to present data collected in the environmental quality survey.
- Traffic counts at different times of the day for comparison.
- Bar chart to present data collected during the traffic count.
- Secondary data research – local crime rates, house prices, census data.
- Comparison to another country using Dollar Street (see www.gapminder.org/dollar-street).
- Photo collage of the local area to showcase the highlights and issues.

Taking it further

Students can then put this information together to write a geographical account of their local area. If you have students in your class from a wide catchment this would be a great way to showcase their lived geography experiences.

Teaching tip

Upload copies of the resources to your school's learning platform so that students have something to refer to and set smaller deadlines to keep students on-track. Showcase good pieces of work at the start of each lesson so that students can see what they are aiming for.

IDEA 30

Sphere of influence

'This is one of our themes for Paper 3 and students found it hard to visualise at first. This activity helped my students to understand the concept.' *Geography teacher*

This simple classroom activity will help your students to visualise a sphere of influence as well as help them to identify and describe patterns on a map.

The sphere of influence is the area surrounding a location that is affected by that location's activities. Students can investigate the sphere of influence of their school and identify patterns on a map as a result of the school's location.

Place your school at the centre of an online map and project it onto a screen. Include a 2–3 km radius from the school so that students can find where they live.

Give each student a sticky note or sticky tab and ask them to put it on the screen where they live. This just needs to be placed on the road where they live instead of identifying their exact home.

If any students live outside the 2–3 km radius ask them to put their sticky note to the outside of the map in the general direction of their home.

Once students have completed this, ask the students to describe the patterns they can see on the map. Are there clusters close to the school or is the pattern random? Are there areas of the map where there are no sticky notes? What might this suggest?

Ask students how they could use this in their fieldwork. For example, could they collect postcodes of questionnaire participants and then map them to find out the influence of their high street or a particular sporting event?

Taking it further

If students collect data on sphere of influence as part of their wider fieldwork, get them to present this on ArcGIS using a pinpoint for each postcode. You can then use the various integrated tools to measure distances and add layers of additional data to build up a more detailed picture of your fieldwork location.

IDEA 31

Virtual fieldwork

'Using online tools enabled us to view our fieldwork location before we visited. This helped us to visualise each location and collect some secondary data prior to our visit.' *Year 13 student*

Approaches to virtual fieldwork have really progressed over the last five years and now there are lots of ways of visiting a location before going there. In doing so, your students can trial methods such as environmental quality surveys, land-use surveys and even investigate change over time.

Virtual fieldwork is a way of investigating a location without physically visiting. This could be through videos, online mapping software with 'street view', or photographs. Lots of ready-made examples exist — for example, VR Glaciers, which enables you to explore glaciated landscapes, and Eden River Trust, to investigate the River Eden. These resources can either be used as a whole class or you can set tasks for individual students.

Ideas for virtual fieldwork include:

- Take screenshots and annotate them. This will help students to practise the art of annotating photographs.
- Use any 360° videos to practise environmental quality surveys and observational studies.
- Most mapping software contains measurement tools, which can be used to measure distances between sites, calculate the area of features and plot transects.
- Use street-view tools to practise land-use surveys and residential surveys.
- Practise field sketch skills for a wide variety of environments.
- Make comparisons between locations. For example at A Level, students could compare their near and distant places as part of the Changing Places unit.

Teaching tip

Use virtual fieldwork with students who are unable to attend field trips. This will give them the opportunity to 'visit' the location and practise many of the skills and methods used during fieldwork. You could set up an ArcGIS StoryMap to share with students (see **Idea 11**).

Taking it further

Use virtual fieldwork to visit a tropical rainforest in Brazil or a desert in Australia. There are endless possibilities with many 360° videos that will enable you to explore a wide range of environments.

IDEA 32

Visit Antarctica and be back in time for break

'It was like really being there, I didn't realise how much we would see.' *Year 8 student*

In a time of rising costs and full school calendars it can be challenging to slot in fieldwork. Virtual visits can help embed fieldwork as an integral part of every scheme of work.

Idea 31 gives some suggestions on how we can utilise virtual fieldwork to complete a pre-visit, but how else could we embed this into our curriculums to make it part of our everyday pedagogy? Alice McCaughern shares her practical suggestions on how she has embedded this into her classroom practice.

As with many skills, it's important to try and embed it where you can, as early as you can. Using online mapping software such as Google Earth can be a really useful tool to support learning while developing digital and GIS skills.

You could:

- visit Antarctica as part of a cold environments topic and walk around the McMurdo research station using the 'streetview' tool.
- look at different (pre-selected) landforms to build awe and wonder.
- follow a river from source to mouth and use the digital measuring tool to measure the width of the river at various points. You could also look at how the relief of the land changes.
- use the 'change dates' feature in Google Maps to examine how a location, such as the Stratford Olympic Site, has changed over time. This could be a good opportunity to practise land use surveys.

Teaching tip

Students can get distracted by using technology. While phones are often banished from the classroom, their favourite apps can also be found on their 'educational' device and so standing at the back of the classroom to be visible can deter them virtually venturing elsewhere.

IDEA 33

Flood risk maps

'Using flood maps added valuable secondary data to our investigation as we were able to add flood information to help us to answer our enquiry question.' *Year 11 student*

If students can bring their own devices or you have access to a computer suite it is worth investigating flood maps as a piece of secondary data. This will also enable your students to understand more about concepts such as risk, inequality and resilience.

Teaching tip

Include copies of the flood risk maps in your risk assessments and the data collection booklet for easy reference.

Flood map data can be used when completing river fieldwork. The Environment Agency allows you to create flood risk maps for your location: https://flood-map-for-planning.service.gov.uk/location.

Remember, secondary data is integral to fieldwork, and it would be difficult to find out about the flood risk without it.

Use the flood risk map to find the areas at high risk of flooding and locate the flood defences. Use 'street-view' software to view the flood defences and identify the types of river management that have been used – for example, diversion spillways, floodwalls or embankments. This will help you to select sites to visit on the physical fieldwork trip. Look at soil and geology maps to determine whether the rock in the flood risk areas is permeable or impermeable.

Suggest what might cause flooding in each of the flood risk areas – are they heavily urbanised or deforested, or is it the geology?

This information will enable students to understand factors that they might be unable to see when completing their fieldwork.

IDEA 34

Frame it

'There is so much geography out there. Should I photograph it all?'
Year 7 student

Framing a photograph is the best way to make its contents stand out, whilst encouraging students to focus their attention on a specific concept, methodology, word or phrase.

As fieldwork exposes students to such an array of geographical processes, it can be difficult to filter out that which is irrelevant. This is especially true when photographs are used as a data collection method – students can be a little snap-happy. Kelly Peppin shares a technique she uses when introducing photography as a method.

Introduce the fieldwork focus or key word – for example, mitigating risk, sustainability or geographical flows.

Give each student a picture frame template and ask them to design a frame which summarises their fieldwork focus or key word. For example, warning symbols could be drawn for mitigating risk or recycling symbols and vegetation could be drawn for sustainability.

When complete, ask students to cut out the frame and its centre. Once their frame is cut out, they are ready to capture some geography with their camera or phone.

Ask students to look out for evidence of their fieldwork focus or key word during their fieldwork. You may need to model this to make it clear. Verbalise what you can see to your students. When they encounter something that links to their focus or key word, ask them to hold their frame up in front of them, ensuring the object or scene is in its centre, and snap a photograph – frame included, of course!

> **Bonus idea** ★
>
> Ask students to design their own pair of 'geography glasses' to wear during fieldwork. Ask them to draw a simple outline of a pair of glasses and choose a perspective, such as environmentalist, a local resident or an area developer. This will encourage students to view their environment from a different perspective. This technique works particularly well with students in younger year groups.

On-site fieldwork

Part 4

IDEA 35

Where is the warmest?

'We run this at the end of Year 7 as part of a topic on weather and climate. It's a great way to really explore the school site and complete the fieldwork cycle.' *Lizzie Battrum, geography teacher*

Leading on from Idea 23, a microclimate investigation is a classic piece of fieldwork, but also a brilliant opportunity to complete the fieldwork cycle through data presentation, analysis and evaluation.

Teaching tip

If your scheme of work allows, a lesson can be spent planning the methodology and sampling strategies. However, it is possible to cover this quickly at the start of the data collection lesson if needed.

Taking it further

Data could be inputted into Digimaps or ArcGIS to encourage the use of GIS in the classroom.

Lizzie Battrum shares her ideas on how to run a microclimate investigation. Equipment required: Thermometer, anemometer, clipboard and recording sheet.

First, spend a lesson exploring microclimates and the factors that influence them (e.g. aspect, shelter, buildings, presence of wind and type of surface).

Ask students to identify four to six contrasting areas of the school site to explore and justify their choices. This gives the students ownership of the fieldwork.

At each site, students measure the temperature and wind speed three times to gain an average. Measurements should be recorded in a table and brought back to class ready for presentation and analysis.

Create a bar chart for temperature and wind speed measurements. The data can then be analysed, conclusions written and the investigation evaluated. During analysis, students should reflect on what the differences are between each location and how these factors could have impacted the microclimate of that site.

IDEA 36

Sit back and look at the clouds

'I didn't realise just how many different types of cloud there were.'
Year 7 student

Whilst students won't collect data during this activity, this is a fun idea for teaching the different types of cloud and the weather they bring.

A fun way to learn more about clouds is by going outside and turning your eyes to the skies and using a cloud guide resource (see the online resources) to help spot the different types.

- Take your class outside to an open area. They could either sit down or lay down.
- Start by pointing out simple cloud types such as cumulus and stratus and ask students to describe the shapes to you. They could also sketch the cloud types.
- Use the opportunity to decide on the wind direction and wind speed. How fast are the clouds moving and in what direction? The wind speed at altitude tends to be faster than on the ground. Does it look like the clouds are moving faster than what the wind is moving the leaves on the ground?
- Do the bottom of the cumulus clouds look dark and flat? This is what a glider pilot would look for to find areas of lift to enable them to stay in the air for longer.
- Does it look like the clouds are beginning to form towers? A cumulonimbus cloud could be forming, which creates a great opportunity to discuss rainfall and storms.
- How much of the sky is covered by cloud? Ask students to identify the number of oktas of cloud cover (see **Idea 23**).
- Can they identify the different heights at which the clouds form?

Teaching tip

This could be a great introduction to expected behaviour in fieldwork, especially if this is a new class to you, or you haven't taken a class outside before.

Bonus idea ★

Visit the Cloud Appreciation Society, navigate to 'School resource pack', and apply for the free postal pack to learn more about clouds.

IDEA 37

Lichen and pollution

'Lichen can be used as evidence of pollution, as it is a bioindicator of nitrogen pollution. It is a great investigation, and something a little bit different.' *Kathryn McGrath, curriculum leader for geography*

Do your students know about the importance of lichen? During this investigation, students learn how to identify different lichen types as well as where it might be found.

Kathryn McGrath uses this idea with her KS3 students. It is based on a study by Wolseley et al. (2009) and an FSC fieldwork week idea. Before doing the investigation, walk around the school site to work out where lichen can be found.

- Choose areas of the school with benches or trees where the students can find evidence of lichen. This activity could also be completed in a local park.
- Show students what Xanthoria (nitrogen tolerant) and Usnea (nitrogen sensitive) lichen look like. Students should look for evidence of both of these.
- Wolseley et al. (2009) found that twigs are likely to contain nitrogen tolerant species such as Xanthoria as they are more sensitive to lower concentrations of nitrogen pollution compared to tree trunks.
- Students should use lichen ID sheets and tally the number of species they identify at each site. Also ask them to take photographs.
- On returning to the classroom students can create a range of graphs as well as annotated photographs.
- If Xanthoria species is abundant, students can conclude that air pollution is occurring at the area they have sampled. They can then evaluate the study and discuss its successes and limitations.

Taking it further

Combine this idea with **Idea 38** and use this to write to the local council about air pollution and the impacts that it could be having on the school community.

Bonus idea ★

You can use the FSC publication 'Lichen based index to nitrogen air quality guide' to help you to identify the different lichen species. This can be purchased from the FSC online shop.

How sustainable is your school?

'A great way to introduce on-site fieldwork as we didn't need any equipment, but it gave our students a range of different surveys and questionnaires to complete and a chance to evaluate them.'
Geography teacher

An on-site sustainability investigation will give your students the chance to complete a range of surveys and increase their knowledge of quantitative and qualitative data.

Surveys require little preparation and equipment and once they have been carried out once, they are simple to repeat. Carrying out a sustainability investigation is really simple (see the worksheet on the online resources) and adapting it to your context will lead to a piece of fieldwork that you can go to when studying sustainability as part of a larger scheme of work.

- Set students the enquiry question of 'Can X site be improved to make it more sustainable?' Ask them what features are currently sustainable, where on the school site they think they should investigate and why.
- Introduce students to bi-polar surveys, Likert Surveys, litter counts, emotional mapping (see **Idea 72**) and observations.
- Choose four sites around the campus. At each site, carry out each technique and take photographs which students can annotate on their return to the classroom.
- Once all of the data has been collected, complete an analysis of the data and consider the recommendations you would make to the school's senior leadership team about how the site could be made more sustainable.

Taking it further

Students could research into schemes which could be implemented to make the site more sustainable – e.g. recycling bins, time-sensitive lighting and the planting of wildflowers. You could also invite the headteacher to go on a walk around the school site to see where your class's ideas could be implemented.

Bonus idea ★

Upload data results as radial diagrams and create ArcGIS StoryMaps to showcase the sustainability of the school site. This would also enable students to improve their GIS knowledge.

IDEA 39

Soundscaping

'This was the first piece of fieldwork I did, and it really helped me to get to know the school better – there were so many different sounds.' *Year 9 student*

A soundscape is the combination of sounds you hear in an environment – in school this might be lesson bells, playground chatter and the sound of gulls following breaktime! Mapping these sounds is a lovely introduction to fieldwork and map skills.

Soundscaping can take a number of forms; this simple idea can be completed along a transect (see **Idea 45**) or at set sites around your campus. You will need maps of your campus, clipboards, a decibel meter and a sound recorder.

- In the classroom, ask students to close their eyes and listen carefully – what can they hear and in what direction are those sounds coming from? Ask them to make a note of those sounds. They could also draw symbols to represent those sounds.
- Take your class outside to your first site. Ask students to sit quietly and take in the sounds for 5 minutes, then record those sounds and measure how loud they are with a decibel meter. They should draw symbols on their maps to represent the sounds.
- Move through each site. (You could also include an indoor site in a busy area of school.) Repeat the steps of sitting and listening to the sounds and drawing them onto the maps.
- On your return to the classroom, analyse the decibel meter readings and draw proportional circles to represent the level of sound in each location. Students can then describe the differing sound levels. They can also explain why they heard certain sounds at each site.

Taking it further

Ask students to carry out this same activity for homework. Students could take in sounds from their home and local areas and map these in a similar way to the one they completed at school.

Bonus idea ★

Sounds could be categorised into 'biophony' (ecosystem sounds such as birdsong), 'geophony' (physical environment sounds, such as the wind) and 'anthrophony' (sounds from people).

IDEA 40

Ecosystems treasure hunt

'We used this following a lesson on producers and food webs in deciduous woodlands. It was a fun way to investigate what we could find on-site and to apply our knowledge from the lesson.'
Hilary Carpenter, lead teacher of geography

The ecosystems treasure hunt combines observations with knowledge gained from lessons on food webs. It is also a great way to clarify different plant, insect and animal species with students, especially if they are unfamiliar with them.

This idea was used with Year 7 students by Hilary Carpenter and could be adapted for other year groups when looking at different ecosystems. This is a simple activity to get students out of the classroom with no equipment, to test and develop their observation skills.

- Give students a wildlife identification grid (see online resources). This could be adapted to contain flora and fauna that you know can be found on the school site.
- Take students outside to one location and ask them to find evidence of as many of the plants and animals that they can. This could be the plant or animal itself or evidence, such as a trail from pawprints. These pieces of evidence could be tallied or ticked.
- You could compare this to a second site with contrasting wildlife – Hilary used a basketball field and the school garden.
- Students can then take the data they collected and turn this into a graph to show each trophic level. This could be a simple bar chart or a compound bar chart for each site. It could also be turned into a word cloud for your class. Ask each student to write down two words that summarise your school's ecosystem onto a sticky note or enter them on the word cloud function on the Mentimeter website.

Teaching tip

This is also a great way to introduce Year 6 students to some fieldwork during their transition lessons as it is low threat, easy to organise and facilitates great conservations around ecosystems.

IDEA 41

Where is our school most likely to flood?

'Our school isn't near a river, so this was a great way to get some hydrology fieldwork into our KS3 curriculum.' *Head of geography*

Investigating infiltration is one way to conduct some on-site hydrology fieldwork and for students to apply their understanding of surface run-off, permeability and flood risk.

Taking it further

Take photographs of the school site throughout the year, especially when it rains. Use these to show students how the surface affects infiltration rates. You could also carry out this investigation at different times of the year or after different weather conditions to illustrate how soil saturation impacts infiltration rates.

For this, you will need infiltrometers (or the DIY version from **Idea 19**), jugs/buckets of water, stopwatches and a data recording sheet.

- Ask students to hypothesise which areas of school are most likely to flood. This could be based on what the surface is covered in (e.g. concrete or soil). They could also base their answers around slope angles, drains and the amount of vegetation.
- Choose four or five contrasting sites. At each site, place the infiltrometer on the ground (if it is a hard surface) or push it at least 1–2 cm into the ground, using a mallet if necessary. Ensure that it is level.
- Decide on your timings – for example, recording how much water infiltrates in 3 minutes at each site. This can be longer if you have more than one hour. You should repeat this three times at each site.
- Pour a set amount of water (e.g. 250 ml) into the infiltrometer, and start your timer. Stand and watch. After 3 minutes, record how much water has infiltrated into the ground. You could also record the changes every 30 seconds.
- Analyse the findings. The longer it took for the water to infiltrate, the more likely that location is to flood.

IDEA 42

Simple soil sampling

'A little bit muddy, but a really interesting investigation to carry out.'
Head of geography

Soil sampling is often carried out in biology lessons, but it also tells us a lot about geography too.

For this idea you will need a trowel, tubs or bags to put soil into, distilled water, universal indicator and jam jars with lids.

At each site, using a trowel, remove the top layer of vegetation and dig down several inches to gain your sample. Fill your bag or pot with soil and label it with the site number. Replace the top layer of vegetation. Take the soil samples back to the classroom.

Take a small sample of the soil in your palm and slightly dampen it, then squeeze your hand closed. If it stays clumped and stuck together it could be a clay soil. If it falls apart, despite being squeezed it could be a sandy soil. Further information on this can be found online if you search for 'OPAL soil survey'.

Take some of the soil sample and rub it between your thumb and forefinger. Does it feel gritty or smooth? If it feels gritty, it could be a sandy soil. If it feels smooth, it could be a clay soil.

In the pot or bag of soil, add some distilled water and a few drops of universal indicator. Is the soil acid or alkali?

Pour all of the soil and water into a jar and add more water to cover the soil. Add a few drops of washing up liquid and replace the lid. Shake the jar and then leave to settle. This will enable you to see the types of sediments in your soil. These could then be drawn the next day.

Repeat with your other samples.

Teaching tip

Practise this before trying it with students. This will help you to create further soil samples to show your students.

IDEA 43

Five, six, seven, eight

'A basic traffic count can be used in a variety of fieldwork investigations, and it is so simple to carry out.' *Geography teacher*

Traffic counts will provide you with data that can be used in a range of investigations, including sustainability, air pollution, sphere of influence, noise and flows. They are simple to carry out and can easily be completed within a lesson.

At my school we can either carry out traffic counts from our car park or just outside the school gate. You may also be able to carry out a traffic count from the safety of your classroom if you have large windows that face a road. For this investigation, you will need a timer and clipboards.

- Devise a simple data collection sheet with a range of vehicles on. You could also challenge students to create their own data collection sheets.
- Half of your class should count the traffic in one direction, and the other half in the other direction.
- Set a timer for 10 minutes. Students will tally each vehicle in the correct category in their chosen direction.
- You could also take a decibel meter and use it to measure sound levels on the road.
- On returning to the classroom, this data can be presented in a pie chart or bar chart. The students could also compare both sides of the road in a compound bar chart.
- Analyse the findings. For example - in which direction did the most traffic travel? In your conclusions, you could look at where the roads lead to and whether the level of traffic was linked to a specific location.

Bonus idea

Many CO_2 monitors in classrooms can be used with batteries or with a USB charger. Take one down to the road when you are collecting traffic data to measure levels of CO_2. This investigation could also be carried out at different times of the day to see how traffic levels change and how this impacts CO_2 levels.

IDEA 44

Car park surveys

'Practising this on the school site made our actual data collection on our main fieldwork trip far more efficient.' *Geography teacher*

A registration plate survey in the school car park is a great way of practising methods to collect large amounts of data and inputting it into another system to find the answers.

School car parks are generally safe with little vehicle movement; therefore, a simple risk assessment should be sufficient to carry out this activity.

For this activity, students will need a clipboard, data collection sheet (see the online resources) and access to a computer or device following the data collection.

- Show students a vehicle registration plate and the data that they are looking for. Students will need to look at the first two letters on the registration plate to find out where the vehicle was originally from.
- Take students down to the car park and send groups to separate parts of the car park. Remind them not to touch any vehicles and only to write down the first two letters of the vehicle registration plate.
- Students should continue around the car park collecting data.
- In the classroom, students should map this data. This could be via proportional circles representing the number of cars from each location or flow line maps extrapolated from their registration locations.

Taking it further

Your data may also give some anomalies – for example, a car originally registered in a region far from the school. Students could try to draw conclusions as to why those anomalies exist.

Teaching tip

Pre-warn staff at your school that surveys are being carried out in the car park so that everyone is aware of why students are there – this could save a large number of emails later on!

IDEA 45

Follow the transect, part two

'Transects are frequently used in geography, but I hadn't thought to practise transects on-site.' *Geography teacher*

A transect is a line along which measurements or data are taken. The school site is the perfect place to practise transects and a range of data can be collected along them.

Teaching tip

Instead of the whole class completing the same transect you could ask groups to complete parallel transects, particularly if you have a wide playing field. With older students, you could get them to complete transects across other parts of the school site to build a wider set of data for further analysis.

When collecting data along a transect you must start by selecting the route. This can easily be done using Google Earth to view a satellite image of your school site and measuring a straight-line distance along which students can investigate their chosen topic. The line doesn't need to be straight, but starting with a straight line makes changes along the transect more visible to students.

If you want to complete this activity in one lesson it would be sensible to also carry out systematic sampling. The example below uses quadrat sampling along a transect.

- Ideally start your transect on the school playing field and walk back towards your school building. At your start point place the quadrat on the ground and estimate vegetation cover inside the quadrat. Record this. Also include coverage of other ground types such as concrete, sand and astroturf.
- Use a tape measure or trundle wheel to measure 5 metres, place the quadrat down and estimate vegetation coverage. Continue until you reach the school building.
- If your transect is small, you can simply flip the quadrat over and over instead of systematic sampling.
- The data collected can then be turned into located pie charts. From here, students can hypothesise information such as where they think infiltration rates would be highest along the transect.

IDEA 46

Dandelion or white clover?

'Investigating biodiversity on the school site is a great way to practise group fieldwork and to also include some calculation such as mean, mode, median and range.' *Rachel Hawke, head of geography*

Biodiversity investigations can be used with any year group and the range of data collected is useful for practising measures of central tendency. This fieldwork also encourages team work and communication.

For this investigation you will need quadrats, ID guides (which you can find online) and clipboards. This idea is shared by Rachel Hawke.

- Arrange students into small groups and assign them an area of the school site. Each group will need a quadrat, plant ID guide, clipboard and data recording sheet.
- Students should place the quadrat on the ground and count how many species of plant they can identify. They don't need to count blades of grass but could suggest percentage cover if there are no other plants in the quadrat.
- They should repeat this at least ten times and record their results.
- Students could also practise their sampling techniques – for example, placing the quadrat at random or placing it at five-metre intervals throughout their sampling site.
- In the classroom, students can then calculate the mean, median, mode and range of the different species found or have a go at calculating the biodiversity index using the following formula: number of species in the area ÷ total number of individuals in the area = biodiversity index. For further information, go to the American Museum of Natural History and search for 'How to calculate a biodiversity index'.

Teaching tip

Complete a lesson on central tendency before completing the fieldwork, when students then use their own data they will be able to apply their knowledge and have a greater understanding as to why geographers use central tendency.

IDEA 47

Rahn's Index

'Our school building was built in the 1800s, from a variety of materials, and we can see evidence of weathering everywhere. Using a version of Rahn's Index has helped us to capture the extent to which weathering is happening.' *Head of geography*

Rahn's Index is usually used to determine the extent of weathering on gravestones, but you could use it to quantify signs of weathering around the school site. It is a visual technique and will encourage students to walk around with their eyes up, rather than looking at ground level.

Idea 34 in *100 Ideas for Outstanding Geography Lessons* (Rogers, 2017) uses the idea of searching for on-site weathering. This idea takes this one step further, giving students the opportunity to quantify what they can see as they will apply a score to the level of weathering each site is experiencing.

Level	Description of weathering
1	No evidence of weathering can be observed.
2	Slight weathering can be observed – for example, discolouration and rounded edges.
3	Moderate evidence of weathering, the surface may feel rough or dimpled.
4	This area is badly weathered – for example, lettering on plaques might be very difficult to read.
5	Very badly weathered, statues and protruding features have lost their shape and look flattened.
6	Extreme signs of weathering, the surface of the building could be peeling, and any lettering will not be readable.

Ask students to look for signs of weathering around the building and assign a level from the table to each location. It is useful to point out signs of weathering to students and to name them so that students can look for similar examples if they are unsure.

Students should also take photographs of each location to annotate. At least two photographs should be taken, one close-up and one further away to assess the scale of the weathering. Annotations should include the types of weathering and why it might be found in that location.

Give students a map of the building for them to display their data on, coloured lines could symbolise where different levels of weathering are observed.

Teaching tip

Look for areas of moss growth, rust and lichen as these are tell-tale signs of weathering. Students might identify a variety of mechanisms of weathering depending on the materials used to build your school site.

Taking it further

Students could also look at pavements, mobile buildings, benches and play equipment to see if there are any further signs of weathering. They don't need to just look at the main building.

IDEA 48

Variations in environmental quality

'We use this to help our students understand more about place and qualitative data.' *Lizzie Battrum, geography teacher*

Assessing environmental quality around your school site gives students the opportunity to collect qualitative data and to develop their appreciation for their school site.

Lizzie Battrum shares an idea on how to investigate environmental quality on the school site and how this might vary.

We completed the investigation on site at the end of their first Year 7 topic: 'What is geography?' It was inspired by an article in *Teaching Geography* by Kelly Peppin and is a simple investigation that requires no equipment beyond pen and paper.

This idea introduces students to fieldwork without complex equipment, as well as introducing concepts of place, qualitative data, and the potential for creative data presentation.

In the lesson prior to data collection, students should be introduced to the concept of bi-polar analysis and asked to come up with pairs of words to describe a place in terms of its environmental quality (e.g. noisy/quiet, litter/no litter). These need to be agreed at a whole class level so that data from each group can be analysed and compared.

In the data collection lesson, students go to six different sites in small groups and carry out their bi-polar analyses.

Taking it further

This idea could be combined with **Idea 38** and **Idea 72** to create a longer investigation for students to participate in if you wish to teach a longer fieldwork topic.

If you are using a map of the school site to direct students to data collection sites then you can also use the opportunity to recap grid references.

The subjectiveness of this investigation allows for interesting analysis and evaluation even with Year 7, as well as developing their appreciation for their school site.

> **Bonus idea** ★
>
> There is potential for this to be expanded to consider school improvements or designing the 'perfect space'. Students love to suggest improvements, and this investigation could provide data to support their ideas.

IDEA 49

Build me a river

'Make a 3D representation of a river and its landforms to gain an understanding before you go.' *Josie Luff, lead practitioner for geography*

Often on fieldwork, due to time constraints, you may not get an opportunity to examine some of the processes or get much opportunity to practise some of the methods before collecting data. Use your school site to do this.

Using your school site is a great way to practise some of the fieldwork techniques that you will use later. Josie Luff shares some ideas as to how she does this on her school site.

Make use of beanbags, cones, benches or similar items from the PE department to create a series of river landforms and management (e.g. small waterfall, dam, weir, hard rock, soft rock, meanders) on the school field or playground. Get students to be a drop of water that flows down the river channel to help them understand how waterfalls, meanders and other features are formed.

You could then take this further by getting them to carry items to show transportation. Demonstrate that the more of them there are, the easier it is to carry larger items. This can then be linked back to velocity.

Prior to carrying out physical fieldwork at either rivers or coasts, make use of the school grounds to practise. The long jump pit (if you have one) is great for practising measuring the width and depth of a river channel.

Any sort of obvious slope can be used to practise measuring beach profiles. The long jump pit could also be used for practising measuring longshore drift with strategically placed barriers.

Teaching tip

Speak to the PE department before carrying out this activity to avoid any issues. You may also find they have additional equipment that could help with fieldwork later on, such as stopwatches and measuring tapes.

Fieldwork in river environments

Part 5

IDEA 50

The magic of multiple measurements

'We carried out each measurement multiple times. This enabled us to understand the importance of accuracy in our fieldwork.'
Year 12 student

Accuracy and reliability are two key fieldwork ideas. Students must collect their data accurately as this will enable them to collect more reliable data from which clear conclusions can be drawn.

During river fieldwork, students will be collecting a range of data such as width, depth, velocity, and gradient. Human and instrument errors are common, so it is important to repeat measurements at each stage of your data collection. Repeating this will stop students from rushing and the data should be more accurate and reliable.

- To measure river velocity, set up two ranging poles 10 metres apart. Drop your float just outside the ranging pole to give it time to settle in the flow, and then start your timer when it passes the first pole. Stop when it passes the second pole. Repeat this at least three times and calculate the average, to obtain a more reliable result.
- From the left riverbank, record river depth every 10 cm. This will enable you to plot a cross profile at each site. The centre stream depth will only give you one measurement, which may not be representative of the depth of the river in each location.
- Gradient measurements can be difficult if students are struggling to use a clinometer. Carefully model how to use the equipment and ensure that students are measuring from the same point on each ranging pole. Students should also complete this three times and then calculate the average.

> **Teaching tip**
>
> Gather a set of secondary data that students can compare their own findings to. Challenge students by asking them why there might be differences between the data.

IDEA 51

Is the bedload boring?

'We even found evidence of some tiny fossils when we looked closely.' *Year 10 student*

Measuring pebbles and assessing their angularity or roundness is a key geographical investigation, but can we take this further and introduce a little bit of geology too?

Using Powers' Scale of Roundness and observing whether a pebble is round or angular is a standard piece of fieldwork. Students can take this further to look at the geology of the location and broaden their knowledge of drainage basin characteristics.

- Measure the width of the river using a tape measure. Divide this into 10 equal intervals.
- Direct one student in each group to collect a pebble from the riverbed at the start of each of the ten intervals. This is systematic sampling. Remind them to collect the first pebble they put their hand on rather than rummaging around.
- Compare each pebble to Powers' Scale. As this is subjective, the same student should assess the roundness or angularity each time. This will help to improve the reliability and accuracy of the results.
- Does the angularity or the roundness match what you would expect for that part of the river? If it doesn't, discuss why it might not fit what you would expect.
- As a group, look at each pebble. Record the colour and texture. See the online resources for a flow chart to help to identify its type. Can you see where this pebble may have been eroded from?
- Use magnifying glasses to look closely at the bedload. If it is sedimentary, can you see evidence of small fossils? These are always fun to look for!

> **Bonus idea** ★
>
> Look at the BGS map portal to find out more about the geology of your river investigation location. This will tell you more about the permeability and porosity of the drainage basin that you are investigating.

IDEA 52

Rivers bingo

'When we visited the river for our fieldwork, we didn't just collect data, we looked out for different features that helped us to understand rivers more.' *Year 10 student*

How many features can students spot whilst they carry out their rivers fieldwork? Challenge them to this simple game to get them to look out for the features they have learned in the classroom.

Rivers bingo is a simple game that could also be played at the coast, a glacial landscape or any human environment. Students need to look out for nine features selected by the teacher. They then take a photo or sketch each feature. This could be exchanged for a prize such as house points or something geography-related.

- Decide on nine key features or processes that you want students to look out for, for example: interlocking spurs, meander, attrition, hard engineering, V-shaped valley, solution, suspension, bedload and waterfall. Create a simple worksheet containing nine boxes and spaces for a sketch, or set it up on your online platform so that students can upload photos after the trip.
- Set students the challenge to find all nine features whilst completing their fieldwork. They could take pictures as they see the features of processes or could use part of their lunchtime for sketching if it is practical and there is time. This activity could also be built into the day if it is a KS3 trip.
- If it is a KS3 experience trip, you could also make a version which includes some of the plants and animals that could be found by the river to help student to also consider river ecosystems.

Teaching tip

If you have staff on your trip who aren't geographers it would be helpful to provide them with a completed sheet so that they can help students to look out for features, particularly if they are unsure what some of the features or processes may look like.

IDEA 53

Dynamic risk assessment

'Asking students to assess the risks whilst they are looking at them is a great way of getting them to think about the importance of risk assessments.' *Geography teacher*

Risk assessments are a vital part of geography fieldwork. How many of the risks can students spot and what suggestions would they make to mitigate the risks?

A dynamic risk assessment is one that is done at the time of the activity, in this case whilst you are standing next to the river. When students write a risk assessment in class it can be quite hard to visualise the risks, especially as they may not have been to a river before.

- Ask students to sit beside the river and look around without talking. They just need to take in the environment around them.
- Students should then discuss what they think the risks are and be ready to share their answers.
- Select students to describe a risk and why they think something might be dangerous – for example, falling in the river, slips and trips or accidentally drinking the water.
- Ask them to go further and suggest how they think those risks might be mitigated. What could be done to ensure students remain safe on their fieldwork?
- Repeat with the equipment. What issues might there be? Again, ask students how they will ensure that they are safe.
- If students miss anything in their dynamic risk assessment, fill in the gaps and tell students what other risks there are and what can be done to mitigate them so that they see the full picture.

Teaching tip

If time is tight on your trip, this could also be carried out in the classroom by using images or Google Earth. You could also make video clips of the environment whilst on your trip to use with students next year.

IDEA 54

Kick sampling

'This was really fun. We didn't know what we would find but I liked identifying the different creatures living in the river.' *Year 8 student*

Combine your river studies with a biodiversity study and try some kick sampling.

Taking it further

Use this as an opportunity to also discuss reliability and accuracy. Ask students how they could make their results from this more reliable or accurate – for example, doing the same number of kicks in 30 seconds or having the same person carry out the same role each time to make it consistent.

Kick sampling is a method used to investigate the biodiversity living in a river. You will need a net with a fine mesh, a white tray, a species guide (there is a free one on the Natural History Museum website), a thin stick and a data recording sheet. Students will also need to wear suitable waterproof shoes. See the YouTube video on 'Freshwater invertebrate sampling: kick sampling' from FSC Biodiversity on how to carry out this method.

- One student should stand in the water facing downstream, with a second student facing upstream around half a metre away holding the net. The net should be open and in the water.
- The student facing downstream should disturb the material on the riverbed using their feet in a kicking motion. This will release any invertebrates in the mud on the riverbed. The kicking should continue for 30 seconds in each location.
- The student holding the net should then pull it out of the water and empty the contents into the white tray. Use the thin stick to search for invertebrates in the deposited material. Tally each type that you find on the data recording sheet. Students will need to sort through the contents methodically.
- Once complete in that site, students can empty the tray back into the river. This should be repeated every 10 metres along the stretch of river that you are investigating.

IDEA 55

Using rivers for coastal fieldwork

'Sometimes a little bit of imagination can help you to use one location to practise fieldwork of a different type.' *Dr Helen Renwick, geography teacher*

Lack of time, money and transport can make field trips prohibitive. But sometimes using local places creatively can save money and provide students with extra time to practise a wider variety of techniques.

Dr Helen Renwick shares how she has used a river environment to carry out coastal fieldwork.

Coastal fieldwork techniques can be practised around school sites, and even at the river. If it is difficult to carry out fieldwork further from school due to time and staffing constraints, it can pay off to get a little bit creative with your fieldwork location.

Our local river provided the ideal setting to enable students to practise a variety of techniques. With a bit of imagination, a school hill or riverbank can be used to practise:

- map skills
- risk assessments
- ethical considerations
- field sketches
- sampling techniques
- beach profiles (using the same equipment: ranging poles, clinometers, tape measure)
- sediment analysis
- dune profiles, including vegetation, soil, wind speed and infiltration measurements
- longshore drift tests (using the flow of the river)
- beach (riverside) quality
- conflict matrices.

Teaching tip

It is helpful to take photos of coastal/beach/dune sites with you to help students visualise how and where they would carry out the same techniques in a different location.

Bonus idea ★

A Google Earth tour can help students explore the proposed fieldwork site before the trip, as well as review and reflect on the trip (e.g. evaluate or compare chosen site locations). This might be particularly useful for some autistic students and those with anxiety about the trip. A link to an example of a tour can be found in the online resources.

IDEA 56

How does my river flow?

'For students who didn't get a chance to visit the river, this was a great opportunity to investigate how a river changed from source to mouth.' *Head of geography*

Using GIS can help your students to gain a deeper understanding of how river characteristics change as you move downstream. GIS can be used at any time to enhance student understanding and practise a valuable geographical skill.

ArcGIS is a great free (for schools) platform for inputting data to see changes over time, such as mapping how the river velocity may alter over time. When you take individual measurements, you can't necessarily see patterns or change, but when you bring all of the data together you can build a better picture of the fluvial processes happening before your eyes.

ArcGIS allows you to build up layers of information on a map to create an impressive visualisation of data. When you complete your river survey, ensure that you capture your site's latitude and longitude as this is used when adding data to a map. If you collect data in the Survey123 app this can be used directly in ArcGIS by uploading the files.

By georeferencing your data you can build ArcGIS maps to:

- show how river velocity, discharge and cross-sectional area change as you move downstream
- create time-enabled maps to document the changes downstream
- use proportional symbols to pinpoint each data collection point and how the variables change over time
- identify key river features along the course of the river you are investigating.

> **Teaching tip**
>
> To create an interesting data visualisation of river attributes, try the instructions on the online resources shared by Brendan Conway. Following these instructions will enable you to visualise how the velocity changes as you move downstream using data that you have collected.

> **Bonus idea** ★
>
> This idea isn't limited to river data. Coastal data can be used in the same way. Input data such as sediment size to see how it changes as you move from beach to beach. This will help students to visualise the effectiveness of coastal protection methods.

IDEA 57

What is the water quality?

'The water quality was really changeable in the stretch of river that we were investigating.' *Geography teacher*

Water quality will help to determine species diversity and this method will enable you to investigate both ecosystems and river environments at the same time.

Water quality investigations will provide your students with information on the abiotic characteristics of that location. Poor water quality could lead to a reduction in biodiversity. For this investigation you will need a pH testing kit, thermometer, a white bucket or tray, test tubes and a phosphate testing kit.

At your sample site, use the white bucket or tray to take a sample of water. Look closely at the water sample, and record whether the water is murky or clear. Students can also record the colour – for example, does your sample contain algae and is it therefore a green colour? This is a basic observation of the turbidity of the water.

Half fill a test tube with water from the sample and add two or three drops of universal indicator or follow the instructions on the pH testing kit. Swirl the sample of water in the test tube and check the colour against the pH scale. Litmus paper could also be used. A pH between 5 and 9 is best for most freshwater fish species.

Follow the instructions on the phosphate testing kit and compare the colour of the sample to the chart to determine the phosphate levels. High levels of phosphate can lead to eutrophication. A river phosphate level should not exceed 0.1 mg/L. Check the testing kit to see what level of phosphate is found in your river environment.

Taking it further

Students could also create Secchi disks to measure the turbidity. Students will enjoy creating their own fieldwork equipment and will introduce more measurements to your investigation which will aid your analysis linked to the original enquiry question.

Fieldwork in coastal environments

Part 6

IDEA 58

Measuring longshore drift

'Such a simple idea, and very memorable for students.'
Jess Lomas, geography teacher

Measuring longshore drift at the coast or the velocity in a river can sometimes be difficult, but it is fun and memorable.

Jess Lomas shares an idea for how to measure longshore drift at the coast that she has used with her students. It's a classic, but often overlooked, technique. You will need an orange, stopwatch, measuring tape, two ranging poles, data recording sheet and clipboard.

Why an orange? They float, they decompose if they are lost, they are easy to see and they are cheap. If you are concerned about food waste you could also use a cork, but this may be more difficult to see.

- Set up two ranging poles 10 metres apart at the shoreline. Use the measuring tape to ensure the distance is accurate.
- Establish in which direction the wind is moving as this will influence the direction in which the orange will travel.
- Stand one person at the furthest ranging pole ready with the stopwatch. They will time how long it takes for the orange to travel the 10 metres.
- Near the first ranging pole, but outside of it, place the orange into the sea, wait for it to pass the first ranging pole and start timing. Don't time as soon as you put the orange into the water in case there are issues that prevent it from moving with the waves, as this will give you anomalous results.
- Stop the stopwatch when the orange passes the second ranging pole. Repeat this three times at each site for an average time.

Bonus idea ★

You could also use this idea when measuring river velocity as the bright orange colour is easy to spot in the stream, and the orange's buoyancy will help you to retrieve it from the river afterwards.

IDEA 59

Groyne profile surveys

'This really showed us how prominent longshore drift was.'
Year 13 student

Groyne profile surveys are one way of investigating the effectiveness of coastal management strategies. They really bring the process of longshore drift to life.

Groynes are designed to reduce the movement of sediment along a beach and they are a prominent coastal management strategy on many beaches in the UK. By measuring the height of the sediment each side of the groyne your students will collect data to help them assess the groynes' effectiveness.

For this method you will need a tape measure, metre ruler, compass and a data collection sheet (see online resources for an example).

- Use the compass to identify the direction in which the groyne is facing. Record the direction of each side of the groyne (e.g. the east and the west side), as you will be recording data on both sides of the groyne.
- Decide on your measurement intervals. You could use the tape measure to measure every 5 metres along the groyne or select three intervals on each groyne to measure.
- On both sides of the groyne, record the distance from the top of the groyne down to the sediment.
- Stand at the end of the groyne and take a photograph to show the difference in the sediment levels on each side.
- On returning to the classroom this data can be presented as a bar chart, with bars for measurements on each side of the groyne showing the average drop for each groyne. Students can use this data to assess the effectiveness – are the groynes preventing longshore drift?

Taking it further

Students could create located bar charts. Take a map your fieldwork location and add the graphs either using ArcGIS or by hand drawing the graphs and adding them to the map. Photographs could also be added for another layer of information.

IDEA 60

Cliff surveys

'It wasn't just about measuring the cliff height, we learned a lot about processes too.' *Year 13 student*

Cliff surveys enable students to not only practise measurements, but also look at processes acting upon the cliff's surface. Students can also practise field sketches, annotated photographs and observations.

At coastal locations with a cliff line, students can carry out a broad range of methodologies which will not only provide them with data, but also help them to further understand processes such as weathering and erosion.

For this method, students will need a tape measure and a clinometer. Geology guides are also useful if you are unsure of the geology of your fieldwork location. Before carrying it out, ensure that students are standing around 10 metres away from the base of the cliff. If it is safe, this distance can be measured accurately using a tape measure. Measure the height of the person using the clinometer. You will need this measurement when calculating the total height of the cliff.

Use the clinometer to work out the angle between the top of the cliff and the person holding it. Record this angle.

Height calculation: Distance from the cliff × tan of angle + height of the observer

Students can take photographs of the cliffs to annotate them as well as completing field sketches to show key features such as wave cut notches, joints and any noticeable changes in geology. A geology guide will help students to identify the rock types.

Taking it further

Look for examples of coastal management along the cliff line, for example riprap. Students can then assess the effectiveness of the strategy. Remember to take photographs throughout.

Bonus idea ★

Students can also look for evidence of erosion, weathering and mass movement such as rockfalls and debris at the base of the cliff. These could be photographed or sketched so that they can practise an additional technique.

IDEA 61

Geology search

'Whilst we don't do geology at GCSE it was lovely to share some of my knowledge with students and to help them identify the rocks we could see along the coastline.' *Geography teacher*

Identifying rock types at the coastline will help students to further understand why processes are happening at the rate that they are. Being able to put a name to the rocks they can see will help to encourage a love of geology as well as geography.

Many stretches of coastline around the UK have interesting geology. Encouraging students to look out for this and teaching them to identify the different rock types will increase their understanding of processes and make them more aware of the composition of coastlines.

Before you go, discuss the differences between more resistant and less resistant rocks. Give examples of ones you might find at the stretch of coastline you are investigating.

When you arrive at your location, remind students to stay away from the base of the cliff. Ask them to look at and describe the geology they can see (e.g. colours, bands, joints and any visible cracks).

Scour the beach and look for material that looks like it comes from the cliffs. Students can now investigate the qualities of the rocks – for example, did it easily break in their hands or did it feel quite resistant?

Ask them to describe how smooth the rocks feel. Are they rough and jagged and therefore only recently fell from the cliffs or are they smooth from wave action?

Students could take photographs of the cliff material that they find and annotate it with the characteristics that they discovered.

> **Bonus idea** ★
>
> If you are lucky enough to have access to a drone, and have permission, you could use this to capture footage of the cliffs higher up to see whether there are any differences in geology from the base layer of the cliff.

IDEA 62

Coastal management survey

'Making detailed observations about coastal management strategies helped us to evaluate their effectiveness.' *Year 12 student*

Often we look at how well coastal management strategies work, but do we really inspect them? Surveying their state of repair and usefulness will help students to gauge their effectiveness and sustainability.

Teaching tip

When rating the effectiveness, link this to coastal processes such as longshore drift. Get students to look closely at both sides of the groynes and at the position of riprap. How well have the strategies worked?

Taking it further

Use the information gathered to write to the local council. Do the methods need improving or repairing? You may have spotted problems that have gone un-noticed.

Along most sections of the UK coastline you will find coastal management strategies. Surveying them will help your students to understand how they work and whether they are sustainable. A sheet for recording data is provided in the online resources.

In each of your sampling sites, identify the type of coastal management strategy and whether it is an example of hard or soft engineering. Use 'What3Words' to provide a location. This can then be mapped on your return to the classroom. Take photographs of the strategies that you can see.

Observe the state of repair – for example, are there slats missing from the groynes, cracks in the sea wall or broken links on gabion cages?

Look around – does the strategy impair beach accessibility? Does it block off any areas or have accessible features been built in to aid entry to beach areas?

Rate its attractiveness out of five. Some coastal management strategies look more pleasant than others. If they aren't attractive they may deter people from the beach and therefore reduce input to the local economy.

Analyse your results on the return to the classroom and evaluate the effectiveness of the strategies.

Ecosystems fieldwork

Part 7

IDEA 63

Soil scientists

'I felt like a real geographer and scientist doing this investigation.'
Year 12 student

Leading on from Idea 42, increase the complexity of a soil investigation to look at characteristics such as soil moisture content.

Teaching tip

A soil moisture content of between 20% and 60% is optimal. Consider what might happen to plants if the soil moisture content is outside of that range.

Taking it further

Use any remaining soil samples to sow seeds. Which soil sample is the most successful in growing seeds? Use the information you have gathered about the soil in **Idea 42** and this idea to suggest why that sample has been the most successful.

For this idea you will need to work with your science department as they are likely to have the equipment required. You will need scales, evaporating dish, goggles, tongs, Bunsen burner, tripod, gauze or an oven.

Collect your samples in the same way as **Idea 42** and head to the laboratory. Ask students to put their goggles on.

Place the evaporating dish onto the scales and zero the counter. Half-fill the dish with fresh soil and record the weight. You will be comparing the start and end weights.

If using a Bunsen burner, set up the tripod and gauze over the burner and place the soil-filled dish on top. Connect the burner to the gas and light it. Keep the collar closed and the flame low.

Heat the dish for 10 minutes and then weigh the sample, using the tongs to pick up the dish. Record the weight. Repeat every 10 minutes. If using an oven, place the dish in the oven for 10 minutes and then weigh, record and repeat. The oven should be set to around 105°C.

When there is no change in weight you have burnt off the soil moisture. Find the difference between the dried and fresh soil and use this to calculate the percentage moisture content of the fresh soil. The longer it takes, the higher the soil moisture content.

Complete this with each of your samples.

IDEA 64

Blackthorn, hazel, rosehip ...

'I even practised this at home as I found it so interesting.'
Year 7 student

Hedgerow surveys are an accessible way to practise biodiversity counts and sampling strategies. These could be carried out on your school site or in the local neighbourhood.

Hedgerows usually contain a wide variety of flora and fauna so they are always interesting to investigate. For this idea you will need a tape measure, species identification guide (see the online resources) and a recording sheet.

- Select the area of hedgerow which you wish to investigate. Give groups of students 5–10 metres of hedgerow to inspect, depending on the length of the hedgerow.
- Using a tape measure, divide the section into 1-metre intervals. This is a good opportunity to introduce systematic sampling to your students, especially if you are completing these with KS3 students where sampling might be a new concept.
- Model to the students how to look up and down the hedge from top to bottom and how to use the species identification guide.
- In each 1-metre section estimate the coverage of each species as a percentage or use the ACFOR scale (see **Idea 71**). Students will need to look closely for insects and small creatures. These can be counted individually.
- In the classroom this data can be turned into a bar chart. Divide the x-axis into metre intervals with a bar for each species type. On the y-axis add percentages in even intervals.
- Ask students to complete a simple analysis of which species were the most abundant and least abundant.

Taking it further

Hold a discussion on how biodiversity could be increased in the hedgerow if your students have noticed that there are limited species present. You could also discuss the food chain in the hedgerow if you find a diverse range of species.

IDEA 65

Impacts of coppicing on biodiversity

'Collecting data in local woodlands and investigating the management leads itself to some interesting fieldwork.'
Tracey Law, geography teacher

If you are local to a managed woodland, investigating the impacts of coppicing on biodiversity lends itself not only to fieldwork but also improving student knowledge on the management of ecosystems – vital for many examination specifications.

Teaching tip

Before visiting, speak to the staff that manage the woodland and ask them if they would be able to speak to your students about tree species and the coppicing process. Their expertise will help to improve the student experience.

Coppicing is a sustainable forestry management technique where trees are cut down close to their base to be used for timber or to improve the health of forested areas. It encourages new growth, and it is completed on a cycle within managed woodlands. Tracey Law shares her ideas on her KS4 enquiry question 'Does biodiversity change at different stages of the coppicing cycle?'

- Students are taken to two separate areas of the woodland to collect data. One is 20 years into the coppicing cycle and the other is five years into the cycle. The two areas allow students to compare their data to see the impacts of coppicing.
- You will need tape measures, quadrats, species identification guides, luxmeters (or a mobile phone app), thermometers and hygrometers. A simple soil thermometer may also be able to give you humidity readings.
- Using a measuring tape, measure an area of 10 metres squared in each of the sampling sites. Outline this with measuring tapes or sticks. Place a quadrat randomly ten times within the 10-metre square. Identify and count the species present in each quadrat. Discuss with students whether this is the best sampling strategy to use or whether

systematic or stratified could be used instead. This will help students to evaluate their methods whilst they are carrying them out.
- Use the luxmeter, thermometer and hygrometer to measure light intensity, temperature and humidity in the 10-metre square. Students should also record their observations – what can they see and hear in each of the forested areas. Encourage students to take photographs. These can be annotated on their return. Apps such as Merlin can be used to identify birds through photographs and recording their birdsong.
- Complete this again in the second forested area. Remind students to measure their data collection site carefully so that accurate and reliable comparisons can be made between the two sites.
- Compare the results between the two locations to analyse how biodiversity changes at different stages of the coppicing cycle. Students could create bar charts or pie charts to present their biodiversity data.

> **Bonus idea** ★
>
> If this piece of fieldwork is being carried out in a large forest, students could also complete a transect survey – exposing them to further fieldwork techniques. Students could look at how biodiversity changes along the transect or the pattern of coppicing along the transect.

IDEA 66

Measuring the carbon storage of trees

'This is a fantastic way to help students visualise just how important preservation of ancient forests is in the sequestration of carbon.'
Daisy Levett, head of geography

Carbon sequestration is the process by which carbon is captured and stored. Measuring the carbon storage of trees can be carried out on-site or on a larger scale.

Daisy Levett has carried out carbon storage fieldwork with both KS3 and KS5 students. At KS3, she completes this as part of a wider unit on forest ecosystems and the trees were measured on-site. For this idea, you will need a tape measure.

- Split students into groups and model how to measure the circumference of a tree. Measure 1.3 m up the tree trunk from the ground and use a tape measure to measure around the tree trunk at 1.3 m.
- Ask students to measure the circumference of selected trees on your school site using the same method.
- Use the simple conversion table provided in the online resources to calculate the dry weight of the tree from the circumference. Use the circumference measurement in the table that is closest to your measurement. Approximately half of the dry weight is carbon. Divide the dry weight by two and this will tell you how many kilograms of carbon are stored in the tree.
- Students can also calculate the age of the tree by dividing the circumference by the growth rate. Refer to the online resources for a list of the most common trees and their growth rates.

Teaching tip

Students could consider the benefits of tree preservation on a much wider scale. It also allows some opportunities for students to discuss the factors that may affect a forest's ability to store carbon, as well as evaluating the process itself.

Taking it further

At A-Level, this can be upscaled to compare trees in deciduous and coniferous woodlands. Students would need to select a sampling strategy when devising their data collection method.

IDEA 67

Pooters and white sheets

'This was really fun! I had no idea how many species we would find in just one tree.' *Year 7 student*

Find out more about your local ecosystems with an invertebrate survey. This will help you to build a food chain or web for a range of small-scale ecosystems around your school site or local park.

Invertebrate surveys enable you to take a closer look at the insects living in trees and hedgerows in your chosen fieldwork site.

For this investigation you will need Pooters, insect identification guides, a stick and a white sheet. Insect identification guides can be found on the Buglife website (search for 'Identify a bug') and the Natural History Museum website (search for 'common insect and other invertebrate groups'). Phone apps such as 'Seek' and 'Google Lens' can also be used if students have access to devices.

- Lay the white sheet on the ground underneath your chosen tree or hedgerow.
- Using the stick shake the branches of the tree, this will cause the invertebrates to fall down onto the white sheet.
- Take your Pooter and place one tube in your mouth and the other to the insects. Suck the end of the tube that is in your mouth. Don't worry, there is a barrier preventing insects from entering that tube! The insect will end up in the collection pot.
- Use the identification guide to find out what type of insect it is. Record how many of each species is found at each site, are some more abundant than others.
- Repeat this on other trees for comparison.
- Analyse the results. How many different species were found? Does this indicate a healthy and biodiverse ecosystem or were very few invertebrates found?

Teaching tip

Some students may not want to take part in this investigation as they may be afraid of insects, therefore careful group selection will be needed.

Taking it further

Upload the data into ArcGIS to create proportional symbols for each species found. This would provide an interesting data presentation, especially if the investigation is carried out on multiple trees at the same location.

IDEA 68

Country parks and quadrats

'Following Covid, we decided to conduct local fieldwork in order to support our Key Stage 4 Year 11 students.' *Charlotte Savill, head of geography and Anya Evitts, geography teacher*

Using a local country park is a great way to carry out fieldwork, especially when you may have students who are anxious about travelling and the costs associated with fieldwork.

Charlotte Savill and Anya Evitts share their idea for local ecosystems fieldwork which kept costs low and enabled students to still collect meaningful data.

- A hypothesis such as 'The ecosystem at X is healthy and balanced' could be used. Students can then complete a transect comparing four different sites to collect primary data.
- Equipment needed: metre sticks, measuring tapes and quadrats. You could also take this further with anemometers and decibel meters to contextualise the primary data.
- For transects, student will need to complete tables for each transect showing the percentage plant coverage, type of plants and plant height. This will be measured at 1-metre intervals at each site.
- Park rangers or staff may be able to give an insight into the running of the park and the current issues facing the ecosystem. These are often provided free of charge.
- Depending on the time of year, you may want to consider booking an indoor area (if there is one) in order to complete written work or have a space for lunch.
- In the classroom, students should present their data using kite diagrams to show the changes over the transects and bar graphs to represent percentage coverage within the quadrats.

Teaching tip

Apps such as 'Google Lens' are useful for identifying plants. This is a free app which involves taking a photo. Google then searches its database for similar images, which students can then compare to. If they don't have signal in that area or data, students can take photographs and then use 'Google Lens' later on to help identify the plants.

IDEA 69

Studying sand dunes and salt marshes

'Keep it simple! Keep it realistic and find a way of engaging students – this is especially difficult when an off-shore wind is making conditions on the coast less than attractive!' Nicola Price, learning leader for geography

Sand dunes and salt marshes are great ecosystems to explore during fieldwork. Not only are they interesting fieldwork environments, but they also enable students to learn more about an important part of their coastal studies.

Nicola Price takes her students to the north-west coastline for their fieldwork to investigate the sand dunes and salt marshes. Here are Nicola's top tips for using these environments.

- You will need quadrats, tape measures, plant ID guides, anemometers, compasses, clipboards, worksheets and stationery.
- Reduce the equipment to the bare minimum, swapping methodologies between the groups to ensure all students are able to have a go with all methods without carrying vast quantities of equipment.
- Work in groups of no more than four or five to enable everyone to take a turn. Demonstrate how to use the equipment, then offer support as needed. Encourage one person in the group to be the scribe and share their data with the group later – it saves worksheets blowing around the beach.
- Quadrats always need reminders about how to gently throw them! 'Google Lens' is your friend in species identification, but use with caution (yes, I really did get a tropical plant suggestion for sea holly!).
- Take lots of pictures! Students need aide memoires – so encourage them to photograph the techniques.

Teaching tip

Boundaries are important, as the beach can be a deceptive place, especially the in locations where the tide comes in very quickly. Equally, remind students about keeping climbing dunes to a minimum, with no digging encouraged.

Bonus idea ★

Use Google Maps or Google Earth before you go to measure distances across the dunes or salt marsh to set your sampling sites. This will introduce some basic GIS.

IDEA 70

Pond dipping

'We practised this throughout the year to see how species diversity changed in our school pond.' *Head of geography*

School ponds or ponds in nature reserves are perfect small ecosystems to investigate. Pond dipping enables students to see creatures up close and to practise identification techniques.

You will need a small net, white tray or bucket, pond species identification guide, a spoon and a magnifying glass.

- Find a place next to the pond where you can easily reach into it without the risk of falling in.
- Half fill the tray with pond water, being careful not to disturb the bottom of the pond.
- Gently scoop through the water using a figure of eight motion, trying not to disturb the mud at the bottom. Empty the contents of the net into the tray. Turn the net inside out to check that nothing remains in it.
- Use the spoon to carefully search through your sample. Use a species identification guide or mobile app to identify anything you have found. Use the magnifying glass to take a closer look. Record the species found. This could be completed as a tally chart or an estimate if there are a large number of a certain species.
- Once you have identified everything in your sample return it to the pond. Hold the tray close to the surface and gently transfer the contents into the pond – do not tip the water back in from a distance.
- Use your data to comment on the biodiversity or create a food chain. Use the pond species guide in the online resources to help you.

Teaching tip
Ensure that you have permission for pond dipping, especially if it is off-site. Specific risk assessments will need to be carried out as you are close to water.

Taking it further
Carry this out throughout the year to observe how the pond species change. This is especially fun if you notice tadpoles in the pond as you will be able to follow the lifecycle of a frog.

IDEA 71

Using the ACFOR scale

'This saved us so much time when counting different species.'
Year 13 student

The ACFOR scale is used to estimate the abundance of species in a sampling area. It can be used in a wide range of ecosystem investigations, and it is a great idea to have up your sleeve if you are presented with large quantities of plants or you do not have a grid quadrat to help you to estimate plant cover.

The ACFOR scale is commonly used in biology, but as there is a huge crossover between geography and biology fieldwork when looking at ecosystems it is worth sharing with your students to help them to estimate species abundance. The scale is attributed to Crisp and Southward (1958).

ACFOR stands for: **A**bundant (30%+), **C**ommon (20-29%), **F**requent (10-19%), **O**ccasional (5-9%), **R**are (1-4%). The ACFOR scale could be used to estimate lichen coverage on trees, species diversity on sand dunes, forest floor coverage of different plant species and much more. It will enable students to estimate coverage. However, as it is subjective, students should consider the reliability and accuracy of the ACFOR scale if they use it in their investigation.

In your chosen sampling site, model how to estimate the abundance. For example, you could look at marram grass on a sand dune. Estimate what percentage of that area is covered with marram grass and record one of the five levels of the ACFOR scale.

You can also use the ACFOR scale to estimate abundance in a frame quadrat. Place the quadrat on the ground and estimate how much of the ground under the quadrat is covered by your chosen species.

Taking it further

Evaluate using the ACFOR scale with students. What issues might there be with using a qualitative sampling technique rather than a quantitative one. Can they suggest ways to improve this technique? Evaluation is a key component of fieldwork.

Human fieldwork investigations

Part 8

IDEA 72

How does this place make you feel?

'Emotional mapping made me think more about both the identity of the location and how I view a place; I would never have thought to have included this in my NEA.' *Year 13 student*

Emotional mapping is a creative way to capture how a location makes you feel. It is a great way to consider how space becomes a place. It is also a method by which you can introduce proportional symbols to students and test their map-reading abilities.

Emotional mapping is where you collate emotional responses to a location onto a map. Mapping emotions enables students to see how their feelings may change as they move around their fieldwork location – students can then investigate why their feelings might change. This can be completed both on-site at school and out in the field. A worksheet to support this activity can be found in the online resources.

- Provide students with a base map of their location. Digimaps for schools has a 'colouring in' base map which is a black and white outline map of a location.
- Ask students to create a key. This could be colours – for example, red for locations that make them feel angry or yellow for locations that make them feel happy. They could also use emojis or choose to write the emotion on each location.
- If students are using colours, they could include proportional symbols on their map. The larger the symbol, the greater the emotion.
- As they move around their fieldwork location students add their emotions directly onto their base map. They could choose to record additional observations on their sheets to remind them of why they felt that way.

Teaching tip

Coloured sticky dots could be used in the field to capture the emotions felt in each location. This would remove the need to take lots of colouring equipment with you, which could potentially get lost.

Taking it further

Students could also evaluate this as a method. As it is subjective, students could then discuss bias, but also the merits of comparing data within the class.

IDEA 73

Graffiti – geography in a spray can

'Who'd have thought graffiti had anything to do with geography!'
Year 12 student

The location, composition and type of graffiti can tell us a lot about the geography of an area. Something that so many of us walk past without a second thought can create an engaging 'hook' for students carrying out a fieldwork investigation.

Chloe Searl explains how we can use graffiti surveys in geography.

Graffiti can be investigated in a number of ways by students. One of the most common methods is to map its location alongside that of certain micro-spaces in the landscape (underneath bridges, isolated footpaths, in the darkest parts of alleyways etc.). Students can then see if certain micro-spaces have a stronger association with graffiti than others.

Students can also look more closely at the nature of the graffiti itself. Graffiti might be categorised as:

- political
- obscene or offensive
- territorial
- artistic
- humorous.

With these categories in mind, students can find out if certain types of graffiti tend to be found in certain types of micro-spaces.

Finally, students can look at what graffiti says about the place as a whole. Students can ask themselves how they feel when walking through spaces that contain graffiti and how the graffiti itself might define a sense of place

> **Bonus idea** ★
>
> There is an opportunity for students to think empathetically when investigating graffiti. Students can imagine themselves as belonging to different parts of the local community (such as elderly people, new migrants, business owners etc.) and imagine how they might feel about graffiti in their area. Students can then take photos of examples of graffiti in their area and interview people in each group to see if their assumptions about perceptions of graffiti are in fact accurate.

IDEA 74

Supermarket sweep

'We didn't realise the extent to which prices changed throughout our town for the same items.' *Year 9 student*

A shopping basket survey is a piece of fieldwork which compares prices of a basket of goods in a range of locations. This can be done along a transect and can be combined with other techniques to study inequalities.

Teaching tip

This piece of fieldwork would not work for large numbers. Collecting this data could be the responsibility of just one group. Keep a record of prices and then use this as secondary data to see how prices have changed in one year.

Students start by choosing ten everyday supermarket items, such as a tin of beans, loaf of bread, pint of milk etc. Avoid items which are paid for by weight as these are difficult to compare. An example worksheet is provided in the online resources.

- Students should establish their baseline using prices from the internet. They could get prices for the supermarket own brand and the top branded goods.
- Using local knowledge or online maps, students can plot which shops along their transect they plan to visit. Students will need enough data to make a comparison – aim for around 7–10 shops.
- At each shop, they should note down the price of the ten goods. If they are unavailable, this should also be noted. Look carefully at the weights to ensure they are comparing like-for-like items.
- Once complete, students add up the prices of each basket. Present this as a dispersion graph with price on the y-axis and the goods on the x-axis or by plotting the price of each item with distance from the town centre on a scatter graph. Students can then analyse how prices change and whether prices and availability change from the high street to the suburbs and the different types of shop.

IDEA 75

Accessibility surveys

'When you really start looking, you truly notice how many places are still inaccessible.' *Head of geography*

Accessibility surveys give students an opportunity to understand how difficult traversing a location can be. This type of survey enables students to further understand the inequalities some people face in getting around.

This activity only requires a clipboard, worksheet (see online resources) and pen. Students can work in small groups or pairs to look at a range of criteria at each of their sampling sites.

When we completed this piece of fieldwork we had eight sites around our town centre, and at each site students would consider everything in their surroundings. This could also be carried out along a transect.

Give each group of students a different a different stakeholder, for example: a person with a visual impairment who has a guide dog, a person in a wheelchair, an elderly person, a person with a pushchair and a person with a hearing impairment.

At each site, students should take their stakeholder into consideration and look out for what might either help them (e.g. a ramp, wide pavements and tactile pavements) or hinder their accessibility (e.g. broken paving, limited dropped curbs and obstructions such as bollards). Students should complete their survey based on their observations. They could also take photographs of each site to annotate on their return to school.

Students could present their survey findings on a radial graph and compare the accessibility of each location for their chosen stakeholder.

Taking it further

Students could map this information into 'My Maps' on Google Maps, pinpointing each fieldwork location and adding a photograph and information. This is a simple form of GIS and a great introduction to it if they haven't used it before.

IDEA 76

A globalised high street

'I didn't realise how globalised our high street was until I really paid attention.' *Year 9 student*

How many nationalities and cultures are represented on your local high street? Investigating globalisation on your high street is a great way to bring this key geographical concept to life.

Using the high street to investigate the concept of globalisation is a great way to bring more fieldwork into KS3 or for students to investigate further for their NEA.

- Start at one end of the high street and write down the name of each building. You could also find this information before you go by using online mapping software.
- Find out the purpose of the building – for example, restaurant, shop, place of worship or service.
- Write down the nationality associated with that building – for example, an Indian restaurant, a Polish delicatessen or an Asian supermarket. If you are unsure, you could ask the staff working there.
- In the classroom, colour code the survey by country and add this information to a map. Use proportional symbols or flow lines to indicate the frequency of buildings related to each country. An example completed map can be found in the online resources. This is also a great way to improve locational knowledge.
- Students can then draw conclusions from their map about how globalised their high street is and whether it represents a range of nationalities. What does the high street suggest about the diversity of nationalities in your town?

Taking it further

Combine this survey with a land-use survey to collect further data from your high street.

Bonus idea ★

Look at the ONS data for your town and investigate the nationality demographics. Is your high street representative of the latest Census data?

IDEA 77

Shopping quality index

'There was a greater variety of shops than we thought.'
Year 12 student

Retail experiences differ from place to place, and there has been a huge change in the way people shop. Surveying this will help your students to experience some of those changes firsthand.

A shopping quality index looks at the quality and availability of retail opportunities in the town centre. An example that could be used as a starting point is available in the online resources. This piece of fieldwork can be used to investigate inequalities, urban and rural change, and retail quality. You can either complete this using systematic sampling or by surveying each shop in turn.

- Stand in front of each shop and write down its name, whether it is an independent store or part of a larger chain, and its purpose – for example, whether it is fashion, food, hardware or beauty.
- Look at the condition of the store front. Is it well-kept and attractive or does it needs repairs or is unwelcoming? Use a bi-polar scoring system or a 1–5 scale for this.
- If the shop is empty, note whether there are any signs of when it became vacant (e.g. a closing sign with dates on).
- Is the store easily accessible? For example, does it have a ramp if the doorway is raised or are there steps? Is there anything stopping people shopping there?
- Remind students to take photographs if they notice something interesting. These can be annotated later as a form of analysis.
- In the classroom analyse your data. What does it suggest about the quality of retail? Consider data presentation such as pie charts and bar charts for each category.

Teaching tip

Remind students not to use their own bias and to take each shop at its face value. If students dislike a particular brand or shop this will affect their results and they will not be as reliable.

IDEA 78

Sustainable communities

'Applying the Egan Wheel to our town centre made us look for sustainable features that we hadn't considered before.'
Trainee geography teacher

Investigating models and frameworks through fieldwork brings together theory and practice. Use the Egan Wheel to assess how sustainable a community is and how it can be improved.

Often when students look for sustainable features they look for the obvious – for example, solar panels, pedestrianised zones and public transport. Applying the Egan Wheel (Egan, 2004) to a location will help students to consider a wider range of sustainable features.

Introduce students to the eight components of the Egan Wheel (see online resources for an example). For each component investigated, they will collect primary and secondary data. Choose three or four to investigate.

Choose a range of investigation sites around the town centre which will highlight components from the Egan Wheel.

Complete a sustainability survey (see online resources) at each site to provide data for most components of the wheel.

Secondary data that could be investigated includes crime data, local newspaper reports, data on new housing developments, bus timetables and routes and availability of community services. Census data could also be used to investigate whether community services are suitable for the local population demographics.

Students could also complete questionnaires in-class – for example, ascertaining how staff and students travel to school and their opinion on local governance and the economy.

Teaching tip

Other data that could be collected at the same time include: traffic counts, questionnaires, environmental quality surveys, photographs and field sketches.

Taking it further

Widen your data collection scope. Ask your students to create a range of questions which could be used to assess the sustainability of a location. Combine these questions into an online form and ask your school's senior leadership whether it can be disseminated to parents. This will collect a large amount of data relatively quickly and provide an interesting insight into the opinions of other adults.

IDEA 79

Can you see what I see?

'Observation and being able to explain to others what we can see are important geographical skills. Observations are an under-rated fieldwork method.' *Geography teacher*

Students may feel that they know their locality well, but are they viewing it like a geographer? Observations take in the everyday geography that we might otherwise miss, and provide vital data for any investigation.

To expand observations, students can complete an observation record (see the online resources for an example). This will encourage them to look at what people are doing, how they are congregating and the different types of human and physical features in that location.

Ask students to look up from street level. What can they see above their eyeline? What might this tell them about how a location has changed? For GCSE fieldwork themed around 'change over time' their observations may indicate how land use has changed.

Observations are one of the easiest fieldwork methods to carry out for people with good sight. However, an observation does not need to just be what is seen. Observations can be taken in by all of the senses, which means they can be an inclusive method for students to carry out.

Combine visual observations with what students can hear, smell and feel. For example, if they are in a location which is using artificial grass instead of real turf, how does that feel beneath their feet? How does this look and smell? What might the impacts of using plastic grass be? When students start to take a closer look at their everyday geographies they might notice a lot more than they realised; it will encourage them to think like a geographer.

Taking it further

Encourage students to take voice notes or use a dictaphone, especially at A Level. They should explain what they can see in front of them as sometimes verbal communication is clearer than written communication. This will also keep a record of the observations they made in that location.

IDEA 80

Using local transport for transects

'We used our local tram system to investigate a transect. Students explored areas that they hadn't been to before.' *Head of geography*

Have you tried investigating a transect using public transport? If you have a smaller group or can divide your cohort into smaller groups, using your local transport system is a great way to look at changes across your town.

Your local public transport system will enable you to investigate a much larger area than if you were just travelling on foot. If you live somewhere with a tram, underground or metro system, or more than one train station you can investigate how quality of life, services and perceptions change as you progress through each stop. You can also use local buses.

Contact your local public transport office to find out the cost of day tickets for your students. Often, group saver tickets for schools are available and these are more cost-effective than buying tickets on the day.

Start your investigation at the first stop on the line. Collect the data you require for your investigation. Remember that numerical data can then be uploaded into ArcGIS to show changes along the transect. Aim to collect both quantitative and qualitative data.

Alight at each of your chosen stops, collecting the same set of data from each location. What changes can students see? Is this expected? Continue collecting data until you reach your final destination.

On returning to the classroom, analyse the data. What changes over each stage of your transect? What reasons are there for this?

> **Bonus idea** ★
>
> Challenge your students to upload their data to an ArcGIS Storymap. This will give them an opportunity to have a completely mapped version of their data. This can then be used as secondary data for the next cohort.

IDEA 81

Pedestrian counts

'Isn't it time we push our students beyond just counting people in a high street? It just feels like it's a bit simple for A Level ....'
Head of geography

A pedestrian count is a simple piece of data collection. Footfall data is an indication of how many people may use a defined space. With some straightforward changes to the way the data is collected, a more sophisticated set of data can be recorded.

Chloe Searl shares how she expands upon a traditional pedestrian count. Students typically stand in one area and count how many people pass them in a set time, usually 5 minutes. This might be repeated at different times of the day to create a broader picture of how busy a place is, or two or more different sites might be surveyed to allow students to carry out a place comparison.

Traditional pedestrian counts will only focus on the number of people seen – i.e. a single figure assigned to a particular place and time. However, there is nothing to stop students from designing their pedestrian count so that additional sub-categories are also surveyed, such as how many pedestrians:

- belong to different age groups or life stages (teenage, working age, retired etc.)
- are occupied with different activities (passing through, shopping, working etc.)
- have accessibility needs (wheelchair users, users of mobility aids etc.)
- appear to be in different group sizes (alone, couples, families etc.).

Students should choose these categories with purpose: the set of categories that are chosen should clearly reflect the type of conclusion that the student intends to make.

Teaching tip

It is important that teachers and students embrace and be honest about the level of subjectivity that comes from applying these categories to people that are being observed. Make sure students appreciate how their own ideas and possible prejudices might affect the results they get.

IDEA 82

Oral geographies

'Interviewing local residents as part of our NEA and collecting their oral geographies enabled us to have a greater depth of understanding of how local culture had changed.' *Year 12 student*

Oral geography is the collection and study of geographical information using audio and video data collection techniques. This type of data collection is a way of documenting lived experience to develop a greater understanding of place and change.

Teaching tip

Check out the 'Voices Project' to find out more about oral geographies and how they could be used in the classroom and for fieldwork, as well as taking a decolonial approach to geography: www.thevoicesproject.co.uk.

Oral geographies are an excellent way to document individual voices on either an issue or their experience in a particular location, for example recording stories about place, change, redevelopment, migration and economic development.

To collect this data you will need to reach out to people in the community. These could include family members, local business owners or councillors. Encourage students to select voices that will add depth to their investigation.

Interviewers will ask questions, but also need to listen carefully and let the interviewee share their story. Whilst this is time-consuming, the stories will provide depth to investigations and vital firsthand knowledge. It also centres voices that otherwise may not be heard.

An example might be asking a family member who is a first-generation migrant about their experiences of moving to the UK, how their lifestyle may have changed since moving here and the importance of their heritage. The transcript of this can then be analysed.

Students need permission to record the conversations and must make it clear how the data will be used. This is good experience for any students who go on to use similar methods at university.

IDEA 83

Perception of safety for women and girls

'We have completed fieldwork with our Year 9s on the safety of women and girls in public spaces, taking into account ethical dimensions such as the inclusion of different languages when completing surveys.' *Briley Habib, geography teacher*

It can be difficult to understand how safe other people feel in public areas without taking a moment to observe the surroundings and collecting views. This fieldwork activity is one way to do this.

Briley Habib has kindly shared one piece of fieldwork that she completes with her students, investigating Emirgan Park in Istanbul as a safe space for women and girls. This could be copied in your locality using the same fieldwork techniques.

- Select multiple sites in the local park from which you can ascertain the perception of safety for women and girls. At each site, bi-polar surveys could be used to investigate student's opinions on the safety of the location.
- Toilet observations could be completed to judge whether they are in a well-lit and secure location.
- Students could also carry out perception questionnaires to determine if women feel safe. In Emirgan Park, students were paired with a Turkish-speaking student to ensure that all views could be captured, regardless of the language, in both English and Turkish.
- Pedestrian counts at systematic sampling sites could also be carried out establish whether there are more men than women in the parks at a given time.

Teaching tip

Before completing fieldwork, it is important to consider the ethical considerations, such as producing questionnaires in more than one language. This will also help to limit bias.

Taking it further

Students could investigate gender in a range of ways particularly in the IB or the NEA – for example, 'To what extent do gender and education contribute to a person's vulnerability to earthquakes?' Data collected during the safety perception fieldwork could be used to enhance further gender fieldwork.

IDEA 84

Re-photography

'I had no idea how much the town had changed until I saw that photo. I remember it being like that, but it's funny how I don't remember Ventnor actually changing.' Member of the public speaking to a student on Ventnor Esplanade

Re-photography is a great way of helping students see how places have changed (or not changed) over time. This simple and quick technique can be a great stimulus for classroom discussion as well as providing students with lots of opportunities for practising annotations in their data presentation.

Chloe Searl shares how she uses this technique.

Re-photography is a data collection technique that uses old photographs of a place to help students draw comparisons with current observations. Using an old photograph as a guide, have students stand in the same location as the original photographer and take a photograph. Students will need to find old photographs online, or they could use family photographs.

This allows them to see what has been altered in that time, as well as explore how a known geographical change such as a regeneration project or the building of a flood defence has affected the look and feel of a place.

The original photographs do not necessarily have to be very old – they could be from any time before something geographical happened that would change the view.

In the classroom, use a clear framework to help students analyse their photos. For example, ask them to find something that has got bigger or smaller, something that has stayed the same and what the eye is drawn to.

> **Bonus idea** ★
>
> With a copy of each photograph to hand, students can use them as prompts to open up discussions with members of the public. Local residents might interpret changes evident in the photographs in interesting and noteworthy ways.

IDEA 85

Land-use surveys

'Completing a land use survey made me realise just how few building types we had on our high street.' *Year 11 student*

If you want to know about the type and distribution of land use in an area then a land-use survey is a great place to start.

Land-use surveys can be completed in a number of ways, but the key idea is that they capture changing land use along a transect. Data is captured on the different types of shops, services, vacant buildings and homes. To categorise the different building types, students can use the acronym RICEPOTS: **R**esidential, **I**ndustrial, **C**ommercial, **E**ntertainment, **P**ublic building, **O**pen space, **T**ransport and **S**ervices.

Decide on the type of sampling you wish to use. For example, you could record every building along a high street, or record buildings every 10 metres along a road. Longer transects will require a clear sampling strategy.

Students can use a blank Goad style map (with just buildings and road outlines) to record their data. These can be created on websites such as Digimaps if your school has access. Use the RICEPOTs code to identify each change in land use. Alternatively, students can construct a table like the one shown in the online resources to record their data.

Walk along the road you are recording data from and use your sampling strategy to record the land use. Remember to collect data from both sides of the road.

In the classroom this data could be turned into a pie chart or bar chart for each building type, or the data put into ArcGIS to create a land-use map.

Teaching tip

This can be done even in rural areas. Fliss Kitching did this in her village following a transect from her school to the church to see if the village fitted a land-use model.

Taking it further

Break down RICEPOTS into further sub-categories to narrow down the building type when analysing the data. For example, 'residential' could be subdivided into 'flats', 'bungalows' and 'houses'.

Bonus idea ★

Students could take this idea one stage further by comparing their high street to one in a town of a similar size using online mapping. What similarities and differences are there?

IDEA 86

Which way ... that way

'This was a very different way for us to explore, it was less formal, and we found things we wouldn't have seen otherwise.'
Head of geography

Try a different way to explore a location rather than the standard transect. Who knows what you will discover?

Dérive or drift surveys are unplanned journeys through towns and cities. They were first introduced by Guy Debord in 'Theory of the Dérive' (1956). It could be a literal wander through the landscape, or you can use a dice or instruction cards to help make route decisions.

This is a qualitative method, where students will gather observations whilst on their route. This can be in the form of photographs, voice notes, sketches or written observations. These observations are based around their perception of that location.

- Tell students how long or how far they will need to walk. Organise students into groups of four or five. Remind them not to enter private property and to find safe places to stop.
- Identify a starting point for students where they will begin their observations. In their groups, students should decide how they will record their perception of that location and stick to that method throughout.
- Give students a set of instructional cards which give commands such as 'turn right', 'turn left', 'stop, and sit down if possible' and 'look up'. Students should take it in turn to select a card and then follow the instructions. At each point of their journey they will record their observations in their chosen method.
- Students can present observations in many ways, such as annotated photographs, word clouds or mind maps.

Teaching tip

Where routes overlap, ask students to compare their perceptions.

Taking it further

Develop this task into a homework activity by setting students the objective of completing their own Dérive in their local area. They could use the instruction cards or simply follow their senses. Provide a copy of this task for parents so that they can accompany their child if needed. Students can record their observations in their own appropriate method.

IDEA 87

How much is that house?

'Property prices have changed so much in recent years, using this data provides an extra level of detail to an investigation.'
Geography teacher

Property websites can be used to provide a plethora of secondary data which can prove useful secondary data for an investigation. But how could we use this?

There are a range of property websites, each of which can give current and historical house prices. A quick postcode search online will provide you with a wealth of secondary data which can then be used to draw conclusions on how an area has changed over time.

Decide on your fieldwork area and how many postcodes to investigate. You could use systematic sampling and find a postcode every 100 m along a transect or use stratified sampling to select postcodes within each area. Aim for around 20 postcodes, as too few will not provide a pattern and too many will be time-consuming. Use online mapping to measure the distance between each data point.

Enter the postcodes into your chosen property website and find out the current prices for houses within that postcode. Some websites will give you an average for that postcode.

Look for historical records for each postcode on the property website, many will show you prices for when properties within that postcode previously sold. Calculate the percentage increase or decrease and record this data.

What patterns can your students see? Is there evidence of change over time, and not just because of countrywide economic changes? For example, if they were investigating a location such as Stratford in London, is there a clear difference after the 2012 Olympic Games?

Teaching tip

Enquiry questions that look at the impacts of sporting events or regeneration lend themselves to this data collection method.

Taking it further

Ask your students to investigate other changes that have happened in that location that may have affected house prices – for example, new roads and facilities being built. If house prices fluctuate, can students also find reasons for that?

Part 9

Data presentation, analysis and evaluation

IDEA 88

What's in a word cloud?

'What an interesting way of presenting data, I hadn't thought of using a word cloud in this way.' *NEA moderator*

We often see word clouds being used to present data from questionnaires, but have you thought about how else you could use one?

Word clouds are a great way to look at the frequency of words and usually they are used to present data from questionnaires. However, there are a wide variety of uses to display qualitative data. They are also a great way to get creative with your data presentation techniques.

- Use a word cloud to present data collected during a sediment survey. If students use Powers' Scale to categorise pebbles, they could then enter this data into a word cloud to find the most frequent. The shape of the word cloud could be presented as a pebble to be a little more creative.
- Ask questionnaire participants to summarise a location in three words. Enter this data into a word cloud to find the epitome words (single words which sum up that area). This is a useful way of analysing large amounts of data easily.
- Enter observation information into a word cloud. Complete one for each site and then compare them. Are there any common features between each site?
- Combine photographs and word clouds, layering the word cloud over the photograph. This could be used to present questionnaire data, particularly if the questionnaire is linked to a specific location.

Teaching tip

Word clouds can be generated via websites such as Mentimeter, Wordart, Monkey Learn and Word It Out.

Remind students that they can change the colours and layout of their word cloud. Colour-blind students may find it difficult to read some of the colour combinations if the background and foreground are similar colours, therefore a quick reminder will keep this task accessible to all.

IDEA 89

Radial graphs

'So, if each shape on a radial graph is like a layer in my GIS map ... can I compare the different data sets if I lay them on top of each other?'
Year 13 student

Many students complete radial graphs as part of fieldwork data presentation. Whilst they are a convenient way of showing values for multiple categories of data (such as scores in an environmental quality survey), the real value of radial graphs is in the layering of data.

Chloe Searl shares the beauty of radial graphs. A radial graph is a multiple *y*-axis graph which can display multiple data categories at the same time. All the *y*-axes radiate from a central zero value like the spokes of a wheel. Values for data points are marked on the *y*-axis itself and the points are then joined up to create a polygon shape. A template is provided in the online resources.

The shape in itself means nothing, but this is where many geography students stop in their data presentation. To really unleash the power of radial graphs, one should layer two or three comparable data sets (such as data collected at different times or in different places) on top of each other, on the same set of axes. Where the polygon shapes line up is an indication of consensus, while totally different polygon shapes show areas of conflict, something which can ignite a greater depth of geographical discussion.

Teaching tip

Keep the number of categories quite small in number (five to seven categories tend to work well). If too many categories are used it can distort and over-stretch the shape of any plot.

Bonus idea ★

Creating the radial graphs digitally can allow you to create an animation within software such as PowerPoint. For example, if you are showing how data changes over time, each radial graph for a different time period can be placed on a separate slide chronologically, and by transitioning the slides quickly, students can see how the values change over time.

IDEA 90

Kite diagrams

'They were a little bit complicated at first, but once I got my head around them they were really easy to understand.' *Year 10 student*

A kite diagram is a sophisticated data presentation technique that allows students to make observations on how vegetation changes across a transect as well as showing the overlap between species.

Teaching tip

Model how to complete a kite diagram under a visualiser with students following along each step. You could use the 'I do, We do, You do' method or ask students to follow each step before completing their own kite diagram.

Kite diagrams usually display data related to species frequency along a transect – for example, a sand dune transect. They enable students to compare the different species and to visualise which areas of the transect they inhabit.

Students can either draw their own axis, or use a pre-drawn axis (see the online resources for an example).

The x-axis shows distance along the transect. This will start at zero and increase in regular intervals to cover the distance.

On the y-axis add a row for each category. Label each row with the species that was identified. In the centre of each row draw a line the complete length of the x-axis. When showing how to plot the data you can add values either side of the centre line to help students visualise how they will plot their kites.

Plot the frequency either side of the centre line. For example, if the measurement was 10% you would plot 5% either side of the centre line using a small X. Continue plotting the frequencies along the row until you reach the final value on the transect. Join each X together either side of the line to create an identical shape either side of the centre line. This is the 'kite'.

Repeat this for each species. If a species isn't present place the X on the centre line.

IDEA 91

Flowline maps

'Mapping flow lines allowed me to really visualise my data and further understand the sphere of influence for my school.'
Year 13 student

Flow lines provide a visual way to show the connections between places. They can be used to present a range of data including questionnaires, traffic counts and footfall data.

A flow line map uses proportional arrows to represent movement from one place to another. The width of the arrow is proportional to the data it is representing. The wider the arrow, the larger the piece of data.

Students will need a base map on which to add their arrows. An OS map or a blank map from online mapping services could be used if the area covered is vast. If the distance covered is smaller, for example within a town centre, students could draw a sketch map instead. This would work well for traffic counts if the direction of travel was recorded.

Decide on a scale for the proportional arrows and draw a scale bar or key next to the map. Include the measurement (e.g. 1 cm = 20–30 cars). Each measurement will be a range of data instead of a single figure. Plotting a range rather than individual figures creates an interesting evaluation point.

Draw the flow lines onto the map, starting with the widest arrow to ensure that you have enough room to draw all of the arrows. Students may need an atlas to help them to accurately locate the starting points. This is useful if you are plotting questionnaire data such as distance travelled.

Ask students to identify patterns. What does their map tell them about their data and why is this useful?

Taking it further

Practise this technique in other topics such as mapping migration statistics. A range of data presentation techniques can be used in any geography exam, therefore it is important that students understand that they have a range of uses, not just for fieldwork.

IDEA 92

Choropleth maps

'Geography teachers are famed for their love of colouring in, which means choropleth maps are a firm favourite.' *Head of geography*

Choropleth maps aren't just an attractive way of presenting data, they are visual and versatile and enable students to easily spot patterns and anomalies.

Choropleth maps are used to present variations in data, such as population density. They can be used to present both primary and secondary data. Choropleth maps are usually coloured with different shades of the same colour, with darker colours representing a larger piece of data.

- Students will need a blank map showing regions or wards of the location that they have been investigating. It should show the boundaries between each region or ward clearly.
- Decide how many intervals or categories you are going to present on your map. Each interval will be a range – for example, if you were mapping the population density of wards this might be 10,000–12,500 people, 12,501–15,000 and so on.
- Create a key using different shades of one colour. The darker the colour, the larger the piece of data.
- Using the data, colour in each region on the map. Complete this shade by shade to ensure that the shading remains consistent.
- Analyse the map for patterns. What is the general trend that can be observed and are there any anomalies? Can students explain those anomalies? Describing and explaining the patterns is good practice for pattern questions in the GCSE Geography papers.

Teaching tip

Consider your colour-blind students here. Different shades of the same colour can be difficult to differentiate between. Instead of just using one colour range, allow them to use colours that they can tell apart so they are still able to participate fully in this mapping activity.

Taking it further

At A Level, this could be taken a stage further by calculating the location quotient of data and mapping the three classes within the location quotient onto a choropleth map. The location quotient is a statistical method to analyse spatial dispersion and concentration

IDEA 93

Using proportional symbols

'Proportional symbols can be used for so many pieces of data. They are easy to interpret and to spot any anomalies from.'
Geography teacher

Proportional symbols can be used to represent a wide range of data, for example they can be used with data collected during Idea 72. They are a visual way of mapping quantitative data which then assists students in their analysis.

Proportional symbols are shapes which are drawn in proportion to the piece of data they are representing. The larger the piece of data, the larger the symbol. Usually circles are drawn, but any shape could be used.

Data such as traffic counts, litter counts and pedestrian counts can be displayed on a map with proportional symbols.

Students will need a blank base map to draw their symbols onto.

- Students should add a column to their data collection table for the square root. Calculate the square root of each piece of data using a calculator and add this to the data collection table.
- Use a scale of 1:1 to draw your symbols. For example, if the square root for a piece of data was 10, the measurement would be 10 mm. Add this scale to your map.
- Use the square root as a measurement for the radius of your proportional symbol. The radius is the distance from the centre of the circle to the edge of the circle.
- Draw each symbol onto the blank base map. The centre of the symbol will be on the exact location from which data was collected. Measure the radius and then use a compass to complete the circle. The shapes can overlap each other if needed.

Taking it further

Input the data into a spreadsheet, including the latitude and longitude for each piece of data. Drag and drop this into ArcGIS and it will create located proportional circles quickly and easily for you.

IDEA 94

Evaluating methods

'This simple activity could be used with any year group, but it really makes you think about the methods you used.' *Geography teacher*

Evaluations are an important part of any fieldwork investigation. They give you an opportunity to review your methods and improve your investigation for the next time.

Evaluations are where students will look at the methods they carried out and will decide what went well and how they could be improved. These improvements could be linked to reliability and accuracy. Students will also evaluate their investigation as a whole. This activity will get students thinking critically about their methods and how they could be improved.

- Ask your students to write a list of each method they used in their investigation, both qualitative and quantitative. This acts as a good opportunity to recap what they did, where they carried out those methods and why they did them.
- Give students a simple worksheet, such as the one provided in the online resources.
- Students need to decide where on the scale they would put each method. For example, if they felt re-photography went really well and they would not improve how they carried out the method, then they would place it at the upper end of the scale. However, if a method such as measuring the gradient with a clinometer was difficult because the equipment provided a different measure each time, this may be placed at the lower end of the scale.
- For each method, students need to explain why they placed it where they did. Their rationale will be linked to reliability, accuracy, usefulness and the data they were able to collect as a result of their method. Use

Teaching tip

Students may not be aware of any equipment that could be used to improve their investigation, therefore it may be useful to put together a resource which shows a range of more accurate equipment, such as digital callipers, flowmeters and click counters.

this as an opportunity to discuss opinions within the class. Students may have different experiences with each method and sharing their thoughts may enable another student to make suggestions for how they would change this method in the future. This is a useful exercise to carry out at GCSE when students need to complete both physical and human fieldwork. An evaluation of methods from one piece of fieldwork may improve the data collection in the second piece of fieldwork.
- Students can then rank their methods from best to worst.
- For each of the methods with the lowest rank, explain how the method could be improved. Improvements could be linked to equipment, number of times it was carried out, teamwork or issues they had with the method. Students may not have access to more sophisticated fieldwork equipment, but they can still suggest this equipment if they were to carry out the investigation again in the future.
- Students could suggest alternative methods, such as a different type of survey or measurement.
- Once complete, students can write this out into continuous prose, linking it to their enquiry question and/or hypotheses.

Taking it further

If you are unable to get out to complete fieldwork, but are completing virtual fieldwork, you could evaluate methods that are completed on videos found on YouTube. Can students spot where techniques could be improved or a different piece of equipment used?

The A Level Geography NEA

Part 10

IDEA 95

Keeping the NEA costs down

'Four days of fieldwork can be hugely expensive, especially in the current climate. Keeping the costs affordable has to be a priority.'
Head of geography

Whilst overseas fieldwork and opportunities to explore a range of environments may seem attractive, the costs attached to them can be eye-watering. Cost-effective fieldwork can ensure fieldwork remains accessible to all.

Teaching tip

Remind students that they can collect data at any time for their NEA (or internal assessment for the IB) it doesn't just need to happen on the fieldwork trip. The more data they collect from the same location, the more substantial their conclusions will be.

At A Level, students need to complete a minimum of four days of fieldwork, and for the Internal Assessment in the International Baccalaureate students also need to complete data collection. Keeping the costs low removes one barrier to fieldwork. Here are some ideas on reducing the costs.

- Keep fieldwork local. Exploring the local area means you can visit multiple times easily. Being able to revisit will mean that students can collect data from different times and days, giving them the opportunity to compare and contrast. It also means that students will not need to stay overnight or pay for the use of a coach. Four days of fieldwork spread across the year may also be more cost-effective than completing a four-day residential.
- Consider using online surveys with students. Some of their primary data could be collected online to reduce the amount of time needed to collect the data in person. Collecting data from online surveys may also increase the number of participants overall.
- Use public transport or the school minibus (if you have one) to keep transport costs low. Coach hire can be very expensive and often an A Level cohort will not fill a coach. If you do need to use a coach, ask if other subjects

want to come along, for example Biology, Geology or Environmental Science.
- When planning your GCSE fieldwork, there may be space to take your A Level students along too. They could set up their own investigations in the same location as the GCSE students as a pilot study for their NEA investigation.
- If you are travelling by public transport, group saver tickets can be purchased in advance, and these are generally more cost-effective than individual tickets. They do mean the group needs to stay together, but you could save a lot of money booking in this way.
- Many Post-16 education providers have a bursary scheme for students, check to see whether they are able to apply for some financial assistant towards their fieldwork. Grants can also be applied for through the Royal Geographical Society towards fieldwork costs.
- If the trip is residential, consider Youth Hostels or university halls for accommodation. If the fieldwork is in the summer term halls of residence may be empty and often they are available at a daily rate.
- Speak to local schools and universities to find out what equipment they have that could be borrowed. This may reduce equipment hire charges, particularly if you are visiting a site that charges for equipment hire. Audit the equipment that you have at school too; the science department may also have equipment you can borrow.

> **Bonus idea** ★
>
> If you are a small centre or work within a larger trust try and co-ordinate your fieldwork with another school so that coach places can more easily be filled. Schools across a trust usually have a subject advisor or lead, and these could co-ordinate fieldwork dates to make them more cost effective.

IDEA 96

Keeping track of the NEA

'Tracking is an absolute must! I have gone from approximately 10 in my cohort to 60+ students.' *Paul Logue, head of geography*

The NEA can be quite a daunting process; however, with some organisation and tracking this can become easier with time.

Paul Logue has a large A Level Geography cohort, and has shared his organisational technique to ensure that he stays on top of the process, whilst also getting the best from his students.

Paul has created a weekly focus, allowing him to keep the cohort on a good, structured pace throughout the year. Each week's focus will have a number of steps to complete, for example: Week 2 Focus: Geographical theories and methodologies - students will research geographical theory, develop their research questions and write up their aims. Students know in advance the plan for the year, which helps them to look ahead at what is needed so there are less surprises.

Tracking is also incredibly important, especially with large cohorts.

- Set a Teams/Google Classroom assignment each week to help students to back up their work.
- Set internal deadlines to keep students on track – for example, set a clear deadline for their aims to be handed in before they begin to build their methodology.
- Create an internal tracking spreadsheet – this could be as simple as a RAG spreadsheet to track student completion.

Finally, keep parents in the loop. Write to parents explaining the rules of the NEA and outline the internal deadlines and timeline.

> **Teaching tip**
>
> Students could be accountability partners for each other – sometimes peer support and cajoling speeds up the process of getting work in far better than any other method!

IDEA 97

Getting the ethical considerations right

'This is probably the most challenging part of the NEA process for students.' *Paul Logue, head of geography*

Students must consider the ethical considerations of their fieldwork, but this isn't something they've done before. How do we make this more accessible for students?

The ethical considerations are a very challenging aspect for students to understand for their NEAs as teachers often exclude students from this aspect of fieldwork prior to this point. Paul Logue shares how he approaches this with his department.

Fieldwork ethics are a continuous feature of a geographers' vocabulary, and we must allow students to build their own definitions and parameters of it over time before we introduce that element of the NEA.

Get students to design a risk assessment procedure for their area. This helps students understand risks related to their presence in the area and what mitigations are needed.

Then, students must evaluate the impact of their selected methods. If using pre-existing templates, how valid are they? Are they reflective of the area and the demographic that they are collecting data about?

Encourage students to complete a pilot survey to check their ethical considerations.

For physical geography NEAs, we should also encourage students to consider the impact of their presence on the environment.

Teaching tip

Ask some key questions to support students moving their methodologies forward, for example: How have you avoided putting your opinions/judgements onto others? Have you chosen a variety of people of all ages, genders, ethnic groups? How will you avoid collecting personal information? How will you avoid bias in the sources you use?

Taking it further

If students are collecting data digitally discuss with them how they will keep this data secure. You may need to ask your school's IT experts to help with this to ensure data remains GDPR compliant.

IDEA 98

Pilot study

'If I hadn't had completed a pilot study I wouldn't have realised that my survey didn't work until I collected the real data. It was very worthwhile.' *Year 13 student*

A pilot study is a small-scale study that students can complete prior to their 'real' data collection. This will let them iron out any issues with their methods to ensure they can hit the ground running instead of having to problem solve on the day.

To assess the feasibility of an investigation it is a good idea to complete a pilot study. The pilot study will help students become more confident in their methods as well as help them to be more efficient when collecting their investigation data.

- Choose an aspect of the investigation – for example, a land-use survey or a data collection method that has been created specifically by a student.
- Carry out a full run-through of that method. This could be in the same location as the planned data collection or in a different location. The key idea is that the method is practised. Students may find that their data collection sheet didn't work or that additional steps were needed to make their method work.
- Evaluate the method – did it work? Ask students to look back at their written methodology to check that the steps were carried out accurately. If there are differences, ensure that students amend their methodology to reflect this.
- Remind students to make it clear to include references to their pilot study in their full write-up. The pilot study is a valuable tool in developing an effective investigation.

Teaching tip

Students can easily practise questionnaires on the school site. They can practise the questions on school staff to build their confidence in their questionnaire technique. This may also inform how they collect answers – for example, with scales, closed options or open-ended questions.

IDEA 99

How foolproof is your method?

'My mum found it hilarious practising the method in our kitchen, but it helped me to visualise each step so that I knew my method was foolproof.' *Year 13 student*

Methodologies need to be written clearly so that anyone can pick up an investigation and carry it out using those instructions. How do you practise this to ensure that the instructions are practical, detailed and clear?

In the NEA students need to demonstrate knowledge and understanding of a variety of methods and be able to implement those methods to collect data. They are marked on how they explain each method and whilst there is no set way to record this, the level of detail in which they explain the methods must be consistently strong to gain the full range of marks for that criteria.

Students often lose marks by not writing their methodologies in sufficient detail. They need to explain step-by-step how to complete each method. I always tell students to imagine if someone else was to pick up their investigation, could they do it in the same way?

Kate Otto suggests asking parents to read the methodology section. They are more likely to ask questions about how something is done if they don't understand the instructions. Practise carrying out the methods at home. Can they be carried out just using the instructions written? If there are details missing these can easily be added in and it will help turn a weak methodology section into a much stronger one. This can also be practised in the classroom too. Students could practise each other's methodologies and be a critical friend.

Teaching tip

Show students an example of a weak methodology with small details missing. Ask them to carry out the method in the way it is written. Then ask them to give suggestions on how it could be improved. This should also get them to look at their own work more critically.

IDEA 100

Evaluating the NEA

'Evaluating NEAs is easy. Doing it to a high standard, however, is much more difficult!' *Paul Logue, head of geography*

Students need to be able to evaluate and reflect on their fieldwork investigations, but often they find this difficult. The evaluations can be very generic and therefore lose marks.

Teaching tip

Have a discussion with your students about what they think should be in an evaluation. They are likely to give a GCSE style response to begin with as they may not realise how much is considered in an evaluation. Use the exam board examples or examples from previous years and anonymise them. Take away the evaluation and ask students to write an evaluation for that piece of fieldwork based on what they have read so that they can practise.

As the evaluation is the final part of the NEA, many students run out of steam and simply want to get their NEA finished. This often leads to students undertaking a very simplistic approach by just talking about the strengths and weaknesses of their methodology and what they might improve 'next time' were they to repeat the investigation. Paul Logue shares his thoughts on this.

For the past few years, Paul has been encouraging students to undertake the following steps:

- Stop the rose-tinted glasses nature of analysis. What issues were there with the data? You don't lose marks for owning up when you've messed up. In fact, you'll probably be credited for it! Students may be hesitant to add this information to their work, but explain the importance of doing so to them.
- Ask yourself: how representative is your methodology of the entire sample area? If you find that your methodology was not representative, what could have been done to rectify this, and at what stage?
- What are the limitations of your sample sizes? Are your results accurate? Students may have found that their samples were too small and therefore it was difficult to come to a solid conclusion, or conversely that they had too much data and it was difficult